The Way We Word

The Way We Word

*

Musing on the Meaning of Everyday English

Robertson Cochrane

Cover design by John Luckhurst/GDL
Cover photograph of the author by Jeremy Jones Photography

The publisher gratefully acknowledges the assistance of the Saskatchewan Arts Board and The Canada Council.

Printed and bound in Canada
93 94 95 96 97 / 5 4 3 2 1

Canadian Cataloguing in Publication Data
Cochrane, Robertson, 1937-

The way we word

A collection of columns from The Globe and mail.
Includes bibliographical references and index.
ISBN 1-895618-13-4

1. English language - Etymology. 2. English language - History. 3. Canadianisms (English).*
I. Title.

PE1574.C62 1993   422   C92-098201-8

Fifth House Publishers
620 Duchess Street
Saskatoon, SK, Canada
S7K 0R1

Contents

PART THREE

PART FOUR

PART FIVE

PART SIX

To Martha and Bob Cochrane
My mother and father

Preface

There were signs early on that I would have a life-long dalliance with words. Verbal exchanges in our house were lavishly laced with raucous Scottish words and phrases of obscure etymology but unmistakable import. One of my parents' favourite epithets for me was *bletherskate.* From context I took this to mean that I talked too much–and that too much of that muchness was nonsense. I didn't know until much later that *blether* was related to bladder, or bag, and that *skate* was a variant of *skite,* a Scottish word fashioned on the Old English *scitan,* or excrement.

My grade seven teacher also diagnosed in me a certain chronic tendency toward verbosity. My most vivid memory of that school year–aside from turning up for my solo singing performance in the class concert with a severe case of self-inflicted laryngitis–was the supreme compliment Miss Hooper paid me at the end of a spirited dialogue in the corridor. "You're a . . . a . . . quibbler!" she blurted, and stalked away in exasperation. I immediately consulted a dictionary, hoping perhaps to catch her out on some nuance of meaning when we next exchanged pleasantries. I didn't get the chance, because she rarely spoke to me for the rest of the school year.

For a long time, I seriously entertained the ambition of exploiting this penchant for verbal chicanery by becoming a lawyer. My favourite passage from Shakespeare was, of course, Portia's impassioned plea on behalf of Shylock. But the quality of my scholarship was strained by the fact that I hated school. And schooling–much more of it than I cared to contemplate at the time–was a prerequisite to the bar.

I dropped out and became a reporter ("journalist" in those days was considered an affectation). This was perfect. A verbomaniac's[1] Valhalla. I didn't have to know anything, and the only tools I needed were pencil, paper, typewriter, and . . . words.

So then I . . . well, I'll skip about 40 years here. After all, this is a romance, not an autobiography. Suffice it to say that my affair with words continued, and like most liaisons, this one has had its alternating moments of arousal, frustration, reconciliation, beguilement, fulfilment, disappointment, mystery, and gratification. Not to mention endless variety.

Encountering a new word, or finding an old and unexpected meaning for a familiar one, is not as big a thrill, I suppose, as inventing the wheel or discovering a new planet. But it does exciting things for me. Richard Chenevix Trench, Dean of Westminster, who wrote a standard 19th century textbook on the study of words, described me long before I was born. He said: "His first discovery that words are living powers, has been like the dropping of scales from his eyes–like the acquiring of another sense–or the introduction into a new world." The excitement causes an almost physical itch, and the only way I can scratch it is to tell someone else about my "latest."

So when the opportunity to write the WORD PLAY column in *The Globe and Mail* presented itself in the summer of 1991, I eagerly embraced it. It has been a

---

1 I didn't make up this word, as I am sometimes accused of, or credited with, doing. As far as is known, *verbomania's* print debut was in a 1924 book by C.F. Ogden and I.A. Richards, entitled *The Meaning of Meaning: A Study of the Influence of Language Upon Thought and of the Science of Symbolism.* I haven't read it. I'm waiting for the movie.

rewarding affair. And I'm doubly gratified when I realize that the stimulation is not all at my end. Some days, my mail box contains nearly as many letters from readers as flyers from real estate salespersons.

I have been blessed with excellent editors. The first is Jeanette, my partner in many things for 31 years. Her keen eye and omniscient blue pencil have saved me many a time from the ignominy of solecism, naked error, or blatant bad taste. Her sound judgment has even nipped several columns in the bud of ill-conception. When exigencies of the day dictated that even my pittance of page space be reduced, Philip Jackman's laser-like excisions left no scars or seams. The introductory words and headings of each column are the products of his wit and whimsy, and *The Globe and Mail* has kindly allowed them to remain with the columns in this collection. Some have been updated or revised, to avoid incongruous and confusing time references, as have some of the essays themselves.

Two of the essays were not originally WORD PLAY columns, though they did appear in the *Globe.* They are the paean to King Alfred the Great, and the brief biography of Sir James Murray, the Scotsman whose superhuman effort produced the first edition of the *Oxford English Dictionary.* But they are of a kind with the rest, differing only in their slightly lengthier treatment.

I want to acknowledge the kindness and patience of my family and friends who, while sharing the average person's interest in words and language, have for the most part accepted my ultra-fanaticism with forbearance.

PART ONE

*

In the beginning . . .

. . . there was the Word, but it probably sounded more like a grunt, a quack, or an oink. Then we got superstition, which begat religion and tradition, not to mention profanation and damnation. The biggest mysteries of all, however, are conjugation and punctuation. Now it's about time we got down to some serious solecism-searching.

Among scholarly theories on how language began are the "ding-dong" premise and the "bow-wow" supposition. (No, I am NOT making this up.) But what about the grunt?

The sound that started it all

Linguistics is less a science than an artifice. The links connecting many of our modern words with their protohistorical ancestors are often corroded beyond both recognition and any practical use. Tracing the ancient roots of language is at best educated guesswork and, at less than best, scholarly sounding bluff.

In the spirit of the latter methodology, I am propounding a language theory of arguably–perhaps even refutably–staggering significance. It is this: The first word ever uttered by a human being, in any language, was *grunt.*

It was, of course, not spelled *g-r-u-n-t.* It was not spelled anything, because spelling–and its constant companion, misspelling–came into being only with the advent of written language. It was several millennia or so after the first grunt was grunted that humans felt the need to set down their thoughts in some symbolic form, probably by scratching in friable basalt with a pointy stick. I have another theory–that the very first message put down in writing was: "Gone hunting. Back at 5-ish." But that's another story.

The Grunt Theory of Language Origin (patent pending) is not terribly out of whack with other, more professional, hypotheses. And here is where we get serious, even though it may not sound like it.

Some quite respected linguists cling to what is called the "pooh-pooh" theory of the beginnings of language. This suggests that humankind's first words were exclamations, or vocalizations of emotions or physical feelings, such as "ouch" or "eek" or "mmmmmmm." This is an inaptly named supposition because the utterances speculated on are instinctive and primal, whereas *pooh-pooh* implies a certain condescending value judgment and likely was first used by some primordial private school boy.

The "bow-wow" supposition holds that early humans, still struggling to keep their balance while walking on only two limbs (usually the rear ones), based their earliest conversational *bons mots* on imitations of animal sounds. Thus we can imagine the scene of some prehistorical parliament wherein the Hon. Mems. harangued each other with "moo-moos," "quack-quacks," "baa-baas," and the occasional "oink." Some things haven't changed much with evolution.

Another concept of how our species began communicating is labelled the "ding-dong" theory, which argues that our ancient forebears played language by ear, so to speak. Thus the first words imitated the sounds of phenomena around them, such as "boom" for thunder, "crash" for a falling tree, "crackle" for fire, and perhaps a "yuck" for the sound of a bare foot stepping into some animal deposition. Whether prototypical or not, the practice of naming things for sounds has stuck with us. It's called onomatopoeia, and comes from Greek for "make a name."

Finally there is the "yo-he-ho" notion (I am *not* making this up!), by all odds the most romantic and utopian, and quite possibly the silliest, of all the theories. It was undoubtedly dreamed up by a sociologist, with a minor in phys. ed. This theory posits that humans then, as now, were fundamentally community-spirited, gregarious, and cooperative. In the course of a day they did many things together–hauling fallen trees back to the cave community to be chopped up for firewood; staging victory parades or sacrificial ceremonies; killing huge beasts, then dragging them home for butchering, packaging, and freezer-storing–and they developed certain ritualistic chants and cadence-counts to make the tasks easier and more fun. Hence, "yo-he-ho." Sure.

Defenders of the "yo-he-ho" theory believe this origin also accounts for the later development of poetry and music, but they have probably listened to the "Song of the Volga Boatmen" one time too many.

The Grunt Theory (TM applied for) is generous enough to accept that all of the above contributed importantly to the evolution of language, but insists that none of them started the whole thing. I ask you to imagine the very first activity, of several very basic ones, that might have elicited from homo sapiens a sound of any kind. Having imagined that, can you then conceive of any utterance, other than a grunt, that would have been appropriate to the activity?

I rest my case.

In the beginning . . .

They're hanging around everywhere–participles, modifiers, infinitives, whole phrases, and clauses that can make a sentence not only ambiguous but also preposterous.

The joy of dangling absurdities

The Facts and Arguments page of *The Globe and Mail* recently recorded the fact or argument that people who collect things do so in response to some subconscious urge–a lingering protest against toilet training, for example, or as a proxy for sexual activity.

One or more of those impulses may have motivated the auction-goer who bid successfully for Napoleon Bonaparte's penis (posthumously pruned, we are assured by the F & A page). But I seriously doubt that they account for one of my own acquisitive idiosyncrasies: collecting Dangling Absurdities (a little known grammatical term, which I just made up).

Readers with particularly penetrating minds might Freudianly point out the parallel between the object of my pursuit and that of the Napoleonic private-part purchaser. But that's their problem.

All writers, professional and lay, fall into the trap of dangling constructions. Participles, modifiers, infinitives, whole phrases, and clauses can be found oscillating in every kind of prose. But to be a DA, such a solecism must be not only ambiguous but also preposterous. An example: "Smothered in mushrooms and lashed with HP

Sauce, I enjoyed the steak immensely." Or: "Although redundant, the company president said the 250 workers would be offered alternative jobs."

One prized specimen appeared on the front page of a newspaper just the other day. The story, about the overpopulation of beavers in Manitoba, contained this sentence: "To help reduce the beaver colonies, the Department of Natural Resources has even begun allowing novice trappers to learn to trap in the comfort of their own living rooms."

Another story described Wayne Gretzky's new $3.5 million California home, with four bedrooms, maid's quarters, plus "a view of the San Fernando Valley and a pool." With his money, surely he could afford his own pool. Maybe even his own valley.

A pest-control firm advertised a device and, somewhat surprisingly, gave the following as a selling point: "The electronic stake emits vibrations and sounds that are intensely annoying to rodents up to 10 feet in diameter." The question here, of course, is whether it's prudent to pester rodents of those prodigious dimensions.

As far as I know, there is no formally constituted association of DA collectors. However, I do know that I'm not alone, and that my fellow fetishists share the urge to tell others about their latest knee-slappers. There are several language usage newsletters that frequently run contributions from readers. *Verbatim,* a quarterly published in Connecticut and Buckinghamshire, England, ran this one, from a *National Geographic* publications catalogue: "Bird-watching chart/map . . . poster of tips for attracting birds with migration map on back side."

Sometimes Dangling Absurdities can conjure up some mirthfully macabre images, like this one that appeared in *The New York Times* and then in Theodore Bernstein's book *Watch Your Language:* "As reconstructed by police, Pfeiffer at first denied any knowledge of the Byrd murder." Presumably he confessed only after a second dissection and reassembly.

Word Watching, a Montreal newsletter, tsk-tsked at a newspaper for a story that said a woman "had moved into an apartment where she was killed a few weeks before her death." Maybe she was the woman about whom a Texas television newscaster said: "For the second time in two weeks a Galena Park school teacher has been murdered."

Webster's Dictionary of English Usage provides two prime specimens. One is a photo caption that reads: "After years of being lost under a pile of dust, Walter P. Stanley III, left, found all the old records of the Bangor Lions Club." The other describes how baseball player Jerry Remy "hit an RBI single off Haas' leg, which rolled into right field."

As with a lot of things, the best DAs are usually the shortest and pithiest. On my short list of short favourites is the classic: "When stewed, I like prunes."

Roosevelt didn't refer to "a day of infamy" and Churchill never offered "blood, sweat, and tears." Which shows how much we yearn for punchy, portentous epigrams, even if they're misquotes.

Say it again, Sam, you dirty rat

The 50th anniversary of Pearl Harbor and Franklin D. Roosevelt's famous "day of infamy" speech is as good an excuse as any to take a look at the famous misquotations of history. First of all, F.D.R. never uttered the words "day of infamy," although the phrase is irrevocably linked with him.

What he said was this: "Yesterday, December 7, 1941–a date which will live in infamy . . . " Granted, there's not much difference between *date* and *day,* but the altered statement illustrates how willing we all are to receive and cherish words of wisdom that are boiled down into punchy, portentous epigrams, even if the purported source never said them.

Pearl Harbor produced another apocryphal one: "Praise the Lord and pass the ammunition." *Bartlett's Familiar Quotations* and several other reference books attribute this battle exhortation to U.S. Navy Chaplain Howell M. Forgy, supposedly as he helped gunners scrambling to respond to the Japanese attack.

But another book, called *They Never Said It* (Oxford University Press), says the fighting words are commonly, but erroneously, thought to have been shouted by a chaplain named William A. Maguire as he helped men relay ammunition up a narrow ladder leading to the guns. This book goes on to quote Father Maguire as saying he had no recollection of uttering the famous words. In any case, it adds, "The slogan had already been used during the Civil War"–which also tends to shoot down the Forgy attribution.

Many of us are familiar with some of the most notorious non-quotes: Bogie's "Play it again, Sam"; Boyer's "Come wiz me to ze casbah"; Cagney's "You dirty rat"; Churchill's "Blood, Sweat, and Tears"; and Neil Armstrong's "One small step for man." But there are many others that persist in spite of dubious provenance or, even when the source is certain, have been contorted through misuse.

Suppose someone during a business meeting is nattering on about the need for consistency. You decide you've had enough, and you chime in with, "Don't forget what Emerson said, Fendergust: 'Consistency is the hobgoblin of small minds.'"

You're wrong, and you deserve everything that Fendergust flings back at you, such as: "Emerson *didn't* say that. He said, 'A *foolish* consistency is the hobgoblin of *little* minds, adored by little statesmen and philosophers and divines.' The *foolish* part is important!"

The conversation becomes heated. You decide discretion is the better part of valour (Shakespeare, *Henry IV*), and say good-naturedly: "Well, as Voltaire said, 'I may disagree with what you say, but I will defend to the death your right to say it.'"

"A noble, if fractured, sentiment," Fendergust retorts. "It's *disapprove of,* not *disagree with.* The only other flaw is that there is not one scintilla of evidence that Voltaire ever said such a thing. The quotation was invented by an early 20th century writer who postulated that the words represented the French philosopher's probable attitude toward a contemporary with opposing views. The writer's name was S.G. Tallentyre, which was a pen name of Evelyn Beatrice Hall, who . . . "

"Okay, okay," you interject, "stop gilding the lily."

"GILDING THE LILY!!" fumes Fendergust. "Now there's one that really gets my goat (Anon.). It's painting the lily, you fatuous Philistine! To quote from Shakespeare's *King John:*

> To gild refined gold, to paint the lily,
> To throw a perfume on the violet,
> To smooth the ice, or add another hue
> Unto the rainbow, or with taper-light
> To seek the beauteous eye of heaven to garnish,
> Is wasteful and ridiculous excess.

By now you've had it up to here (unknown). You look him straight between the whites of his eyes (?), then let him have it.

"All right, you win. After all, a little learning is a dangerous thing (Pope), and where ignorance is bliss (Gray), 'tis folly to be a wise guy."

All sorts of terms connected with the festive season are linked to alcohol and getting into the Christmas spirits. It could explain why St. Nick's always so happy.

A merry (hic!) little Christmas

The Christmas spirit is not what it used to be, and neither are the Christmas spirits.

Pop down to the local convenience shop for a cardboard flagon of eggnog, and check out the ingredients: milk, sugar, glucose-fructose, frozen yolk, rum spices, calcium carrageen, guar gum, locust bean gum, artificial flavour, colour. Not at all the same as the eggnog of olde.

The plain, unvarnished, un-egged *nog* or *nogg* originated in East Anglia and was nothing more than a strong, well-aged beer. It was not likely served in a *noggin,* a drinking cup of obscure origin and insufficient capacity for serious nogging (1 flagon=2 quarts=16 noggins=2.28 litres, if you want to stick that on your refrigerator for handy reference).

About 200 years ago some health-conscious, or maybe semi-conscious, tippler figured a raw egg would make a salubrious addition to the nog, and–*à votre santé!*–the eggnog. Before long the term included any old mixture of eggs and spirituous liquids such as cider, ale, wine, or, for all I know, Cold Duck, usually served hot.

The adulteration continued to the point–i.e., now–where it is not uncommon for our holiday guests to be insulted with the quasi-milk-toast described above, to which alcoholic fortification may or may not be added. What a way to wassail!

Did somebody say what's a wassail? This odd word was brought to England some time before the 12th century by the Danes, in whose language it was *ves heill,* or "be healthy" (there was likely an implied "or else" here; the Danish tourists were, if nothing else, uninhibited). In Middle English, this drinking salutation was rendered "*was hail,*" and custom required the person thus toasted to reply "*drink hail.*" The latter half of this liquid litany has been replaced with "down the hatch" or "here's mud in your eye."

The term *wassail* came to be used to describe the spiced wine or ale used to celebrate Christmas Eve or New Year's, or even the bowl that contained the heady mélange. Today that mixture might be called a *punch,* a word of controversial origin that has nothing to do with the wallop it might or might not entail.

For a long time, it was popularly thought that *punch* was brought to England from India in the 17th century, derived from the Hindi word *panch* ("five"), representing the supposed number of ingredients. Later linguists dispute this on the apparently unassailable grounds that a) punches have always had a widely varying number of constituents, and b) the word existed in England before the 17th century. One suggestion is that *punch* may be nothing more than a short form of *puncheon,* a large ship-board cask that held sailors' rum rations.

Booze (an 18th century colloquialism for the much earlier English *bouse,* a Dutch-inspired word for guzzle) haunts our Christmas terminology more than you might suspect. Merry Christmas? For 300 years, *merry* was a euphemism for "tipsy." So was *happy.*

Ever wonder why jolly old St. Nick had such a red nose and jocund disposition? One of the definitions of *jolly* is "exhilarated with drink." Bells can be *jingled,* and so can humans; during the first half of this century, the word in American slang meant "blotto" or, to use my father's favourite, "spifflicated."

A distant etymological cousin of *jolly* is *Yule,* a word that may not be as abstemious as it looks. It comes from the Old English *geol* and originally denoted a heathen festival of the winter solstice. By about 900 A.D. it was the word for Christmas and the attendant festivities, a use that still prevails in parts of Scotland and northern England but is only a headline writer's shorthand in the rest of the English-speaking world.

Yule, variously spelt, also enjoyed a period as a reveller's shout. Thomas Blount, a 17th century lexicographer, described one such practice: "In Yorkshire and our other Northern parts they have an old Custom; after Sermon or Service on Christmas Day . . . the common people run about the streets singing:

> Ule, Ule, Ule, Three Puddings in a Pule;
> Crack Nuts and cry Ule.

Since smoking was only in its infancy then, we can only assume that those common people were partaking of some other mood-enhancing substance. Probably fructose-free.

Robert Burns's birthday is for Scots a time for solemn ritual and serious elbow-bending; time to shrug off the slings and arrows of the Sassenachs and other envious detractors.

Roasting the haggis

Oh wad some Pow'r the giftie gie us
To see oursels as others see us!
—Robert Burns, *To A Louse*

On Robert Burns's night, in clannish conclaves far from Galashiels, Balachulish, and Auchtermuchty, ladies in long skirts and gentlemen in short ones will "tak a cup o' kindness" or something a bit stronger to toast the Scottish bard's birthday.

At what is considered a high point in these affairs, an awful silence descends. A plangent drone punctures the stillness, and goose bumps sprout on knobby knees normally masked by trousers. The drone is joined by a piercing caterwaul as solemn stewards, or Stewarts, parade amongst the plaid-clad assemblage. They bear aloft a tray or board, upon which reposes a large, steaming tumescence known as *The Haggis.*

Delicacy forbids more detail here. Suffice it to say that some tartaned swell reads a poem by this Burns chap, a poem actually dedicated to the execrable entrée, after which many more toasts are drunk to the late bard himself.

What is there to say about a people who, first of all, can't decide on a national adjective (Scots? Scotch?

Scottish?); second, have a large, prickly weed as their national flower; third, pay homage to a dish made of sheep's entrails; and fourth, venerate a guy who apparently gained fame by writing verse about vermin, while his counterparts elsewhere were celebrating such ennobling creatures as skylarks and nightingales.

Maybe that's the introspective question Burns himself was getting at in the passage cited above. Unfortunately, he lived too early to avail himself of *Bartlett's Familiar Quotations,* or he would have found, tucked between "Scorpion" and "Scoundrel" in the index, some clues about how others have viewed his country and countrymen.

Samuel Johnson was perhaps the most famous–and frequent–denigrator. In an 18th century version of Lenin's dictum about the malleability of youth, Johnson said, "Much may be made of a Scotchman if he be caught young." He had in mind Lord Mansfield who, while born in Perthshire, was educated at Westminster and Oxford, and became one of Britain's foremost jurists.

To rub it in, Johnson was quoted on another occasion as saying, "The noblest prospect which a Scotchman ever sees is the high road that leads to England."

Food doesn't fare well in the comments from other sources. Francis Grose, in his *Dictionary of the Vulgar Tongue,* defined Scotch chocolate as "brimstone and milk." To William Clarke Russell, who wrote *Sailor's Language,* Scotch coffee was "hot water flavoured with burnt biscuit." A character in *Tylney Hall,* by Thomas Hood, was obviously not looking forward to dinner at a Scotsman's home when he said, "We shall have an ounce of mutton swimming in a tureen of barley water–I've heard of their Scotch broths."

Scottish skills are not greatly admired either. Bishop James Pilkington rated marksmanship low when he explained in 1585 that "if any shoot ill-favouredly, we saie he shooteth like a Scott." And the *St. James's Gazette* reported that poor sailing is "what the sailors call 'Scotch seamanship,' which is all stupidity and main strength."

In the *Essays of Elia,* Charles Lamb put in his tuppence-worth with this: "I have been trying all my life to like Scotchmen, and am obliged to desist from the experiment in despair."

Excuse me, the phone. "I've just been readin' yoor colyoom, ye glaiket, skelly-eyed bizzem!" rasps a thistle-encrusted voice. "Can ye no find a nice word tae say aboot yoor ancesters?"

"I certainly can," I reply. "I've always thought that one of the great strengths of my ethnic brethren (and sistren) was their indomitable sense of humour."

"Aye," says the burdocky baritone, mollified. "Huv ye haird the wan aboot the Sassenach, the Welshman, and the . . . ?"

Let's give the last word to the justly celebrated Rabbie Burns. In *The Cotter's Saturday Night* he describes the simple bliss of Highland life. The weary farmer forgets his toil when he comes home to his children, his fireside, and "his thrifty wifie's smile." A supper of "halesome parritch" and "weel-hained kebbuck fell" (sharp cheese) is ended with a prayer of thanksgiving, and Burns sums up:

> From scenes like these old Scotia's grandeur springs,
> That makes her loved at home, revered abroad.

Well, *some* places abroad.

Note: This column attracted more mail than any other. Some thought I was insulting all Scots, including Robert Burns. Most took it in the jocular vein in which it was intended. Some astutely and correctly detected a certain pride in my Scottish heritage. One reader pointed out that "bizzem," a dialect word based on besom, or "broom," denotes a somewhat dishevelled female. The reader suggested bachle as an alternative. I accept the suggestion.

We all know that every fourth year has an extra day, but do we know why? And, by the way, why do all those young men run for cover?

*

Looking at why we leap

Scrabbling around for something trenchant to say about leap year, I chanced upon a quotation from Jonathan Swift, curmudgeonly cleric and dour doyen of 18th century English satirists.

Reasoning that any attempt to improve on the razor wit and laser lampoonery of the irascible reverend would be an unparalleled example of painting the lily, I opted to purloin unabashedly from Swift's own inimitable treatment of the subject–the subject being, if you happen to have lost the thread already, leap year. So here it is, in full, from Swift's *Journal to Stella,* February 29, 1712:

> "This is leap year, and this is leap day."

What more can you say? Except that *leap year* is one of those expressions we so frequently use without pausing to consider their origin and meaning. In this case it may be just as well, because nobody seems to know its origin, and its meaning is a matter of considerable conjecture, much of it silly.

The *OED*'s oldest written captive is dated 1387. It's from the late medieval bestseller *Polycronicon Ranulphi Higden,* translated by the Cornishman John of Trevisa, and a singularly unhelpful contribution to this discussion it is: "That tyme Iulius amended the kalendar, and fonde the cause of the lepe yere." For this they named a month after him, the one following Iune.

As for meaning, at first glance the expression just doesn't add up. If we subtracted a day from the calendar every four years, thereby "leaping" over it by omitting it, the imagery might hang together. On the other hand, within a few dozen generations we'd be wearing mittens, mufflers, and mukluks in August, and mowing lawns and mulching marigolds on Boxing Day.

A second glance likewise does little to advance comprehension. What we are doing in this whole affair is following, with ovine obedience, a 2,000-year-old tradition based on the whim of some toga-clad tyrant who, if he had to meddle with calendars, would have been better off cancelling the ides of March. The upshot is that every four years, without so much as a how d'you do, let alone a why d'we do, we add a day to the calendar. And we do this not by prolonging a languid summer weekend, but by extending by a full 24 hours the most wretched month of the year. The only leap this is likely to inspire is off the nearest cliff.

So what does it all mean? The *OED* makes a valiant but ultimately unilluminating (and quite possibly prurient) stab at a definition: "**leap year**. A year having one day (now Feb. 29) more than the common year; a bissextile year."

Hmmmm. Bissextile? It may be a leap in the dark, but is there a possible connection here with the ancient tradition that permitted women to propose marriage during leap year? In Scotland, it was more than a tradition, according to Cobham Brewer's *Dictionary of Phrase and Fable.* In 1228 (a leap year), the Scottish Parliament passed a law allowing each "maiden ladee of baith high and lowe estait" to pop the question during every fourth year. If the proposee refused, he had to show he was "betrothit to anither woman" or else pay a fine "in the sum of ane hundridty pundes, or less, as his estait may bee."

In Irish lore, the recalcitrant bridegroom-designate had to give the unrequited suitress a kiss and a silk gown. A modern and much less romantic version, based on a character from Al Capp's *L'il Abner* comic strip, is Sadie Hawkins Day.

Alas, the real meaning of *bissextile* is both unconnected and unexciting. For some reason the Romans called February 24 the "sextile" or sixth day before March (this doesn't add up either, but this is the story, and I'm sticking with it). In a leap year, or *annus bissextilis,* this day was counted twice *(bis)*, and was known as *dies bissextus,* which later became February 29.

In ordinary years, Monday in one year will be Tuesday in the next year and Wednesday in the next. In the fourth year we skip over Thursday to Friday. The result, as Sir George Wharton wrote in his 1681 *Discourse on Years and Months* was that "by this addition . . . the Fixed Holy-days, and the like, do as it were leap one day farther into the week."

And with that, I think I'll leap to a conclusion.

Eastertide is the time of year when all sorts of odd terms crop up, such as "shrove" and "maundy" and the like. But the oddest name in the roster is surely the word "Easter" itself.

In your pagan-goddess bonnet . . .

And how are you, this Shitten Saturday?

No, that's not a scatological observation about the weather, or a reflection of a liverish humour at this end. It is an old East Anglian name for the Saturday between Good Friday and Easter Sunday. A corruption of "Shut-in-Saturday," it's an allusion to the period in which Christ's body remained sealed in the tomb.

The great Christian festival of Eastertide has given us many strange words. Some, like *Shitten Saturday,* were regional dialect words, and are now obsolete even on their local stamping ground. Others display a vigorous viability, as durable as the story of Easter itself. We use them familiarly if not ritually every year, even though we may not have a clue about their ancestry.

Before Eastertide rolls in, there's Shrovetide, which includes Quinquagesima Sunday (50 days before Easter) and Shrove Monday and Tuesday. *Shrove* is an archaic past tense of the verb *shrive,* to hear confession or to impose penance. An otherwise archaic noun, *shrift,* survives in the modern metaphor "to give short shrift." Originally this referred to the brief time allowed a condemned criminal to make confession before being executed.

For all its sombre overtones, Shrovetide was a period of feasting and merry-making–a last hurrah before the long fast of Lent. In some Latin cultures these celebrations have reached bacchanalian proportions. In Britain, and its former colonies, the revelry now consists of having a big feed of pancakes or, for the really frolicsome, racing back and forth with a skilletful of them. This low-key carousal is a holdover from the custom of using up butter and eggs before the fast.

Things were not always so subdued. In one quaint custom, a toothsome rooster was designated the Shrovetide Cock. The lucky nominee was then cudgelled or stoned to death, and its savaged but apparently still savorous remains awarded to the person deemed to have dealt the most telling blows.

In the English capital, young ruffians called London Prentices donned cloaks of piety and roamed the red-light districts vandalizing bawdy-houses and terrorizing the occupants. So rowdy was the general Shrovetide behaviour that Bishop Hugh Latimer in 1537 described a group of year-round miscreants thus: "They live every day as though al their life were a shrovynge tyme [sic]."

Behaviour turned from loose to fast on Ash Wednesday–named after Pope Gregory began the custom of sprinkling ashes on penitents' heads to remind them of their mortality. In Scotland and Northern England, the fourth Lenten Sunday was known as Carlin Sunday, *carline* being a Norse-derived word for an old woman. Elsewhere it became "Mothering Sunday" when the far-flung family visited Mum. Our non-Lenten Mother's Day is an extension.

A week before Easter comes Palm Sunday, marking Christ's triumphal arrival at Jerusalem. Palms being scarce in England, branches of yew and other arboreal incongruities were used to recreate the celebration.

Maundy Thursday commemorates the Last Supper, when Christ washed the apostles' feet. He also issued a "new commandment" (in Latin, *mandatum novum*), to love one another. From *mandatum* came the Old French *mandé,* and from that the English *maundy.* The distribution of "maundy money" by the British monarch has replaced the custom of washing poor people's feet.

Good Friday seems a misnomer for the most solemn day of the Christian calendar, but "good" in this sense means holy or pious, as in the "Good Book." In Cheshire the day is still sometimes called "Care Friday," from the old English *caru,* sorrow or lamentation. The holy day is still known by the cognate *Karfreitag* in German.

Which brings us to Easter–surely the oddest name in the entire roster. In virtually every other European language, the word for the day of Christ's resurrection is based on the Latin *pascha,* which derived from the Hebrew *pesah,* or Passover. Easter probably comes from *Eostre,* the name of a pagan goddess of the dawn, whose festival was celebrated at the vernal equinox.

It was not uncommon for early Christian converts in Britain to keep allotheistic names for their new feasts. *Yule,* originally the name for a heathen festival, was used for Christmas for at least 500 years before *Christmas* itself became the favoured term.

Something similar could happen to the paganistic Easter in time. But then, maybe I'm just talking through my bonnet.

There are signs about that we are on the threshold of a kinder, gentler era of pseudo-swear-words and quasi-profanities. Egad! This could give new life to some favourite old imprecations.

Frankly, my dear, I don't give a dang

The headline on the boat-show ad was nearly nine centimetres tall and it spread clear across the top of the page of a large newspaper. But for all its bulk, it had the impact of a slap on the phizzog with an overboiled linguina. Starkly stultifying, it said: "DARN THE TORPEDOES," and under that, "FULL SPEED AHEAD."

Was this, I wondered, the work of a late 20th century reincarnation of Dr. Thomas Bowdler, the pre-Victorian prude who published an expurgated collection of Shakespeare's works "in which those words and expressions are omitted which cannot with propriety be read aloud in a family."

A few days later, Gary Larsen's *Far Side* cartoon depicted a street full of terminally apathetic people wandering about in what the caption described as "the Village of the Darned."

It's a well-known fact that ad writers and cartoonists have always been on the cusp of the bow wave of the leading edge of sociolinguistic evolution, their antennae finely tuned to every nuance, every blip of change at the verbal interface. So unless I misinterpret the evidence, we are on the threshold of a kinder, gentler, smarmier era of quasi-profanities, swearing, and cussing. Damning with faint phrase, as it were.

That being the case, we can't stop with just cleaning up the bodacious "full speed ahead" order given by Adm. David Farragut during the Battle of Mobile Bay. Copies of *Gone With the Wind* will have to be dubbed so that Rhett Butler says, "Frankly, my dear, I don't give a dang." General Sherman's speech to a graduating class must be edited to reflect that "War is heck." Milton's *Paradise Lost* should speak of all "hades" breaking loose, and Lady Macbeth will exclaim, "Out dratted spot! out I say!" And of course, when we're in a no-win situation, we'll be "dashed if we do, and dashed if we don't."

The upside of this mellifluous movement is that it may signal a new career for some splendid old quasi-profanities that allowed earlier generations of English speakers to cuss (a euphemism for "curse") with impunity.

Your basic bowdlerized blasphemy, of course, involves variations on *God.* They include *gad, egad, gawd, gosh (almighty), golly, dad-burned, ohmigosh,* and *ohmigawd.* They sometimes take a *by,* as in a real oath, and come out as *by Jove, by Jupiter, by George, by Godfrey, by Gum, by Gar, begad* and, in Irish, *begorrah.* There is a theory that *bigot* is the result of a similar perversion.

Good grief, good gravy, for goodness' sake, great Scott, great guns, and *great Caesar's ghost* are all attempts to take the Maker's name in vain without actually offending Him–or others. The frivolous-sounding *drat* derives from a particularly nasty old imprecation, *(may) God rot (it)! Gor* (or *Cor) blimey* was a self-malediction meaning *(may) God blind me.*

There is a similar slew of polite profanities based on Christ's name. They range from the simple *gee, jeepers (creepers), jiminy (cricket, Christmas), criminy, cripes, kee-rist* to the more complex *gee whiz* (from *Jee-ziz?*), *gee whillikers, Judas priest,* and *by jingo* (the modern *jingoism* derives from the use of the euphemism in a bellicose, 19th century English song)–and, of course, the Irish *bejabbers.*

Marry, a vituperative variant on the Virgin's name, became so common as an exclamation of surprise by the 16th century that most users didn't realize they were blaspheming.

The really arcane classics are related to Christ's death. *Gadzooks,* an obsolete exclamation that looks comical today, was a contraction of "God's hooks" (a reference to the nails in Christ's hands and feet). *Zounds* and *Gadzoons,* also redolent of olde English indignation, were short for "God's wounds." Contraction, as in *zblood* and *strewth* ("God's truth"), served not only to give a punchier imprecation, but also to further disguise the underlying profanity.

Dropping the first letter in the Creator's name was a favourite fudge that gave us such oddities as *ods bodikins* ("God's dear little body") and *ods fish* (flesh).

The convention of dropping or changing letters, and squeezing word parts together, was known as mincing oaths, and sometimes resulted in such highfalutin compounds as *damphoole.* The whole business was known as "cheating the devil," about whom I'll have more to say later.

Well, the Devil certainly occupies a place of some prominence in the hearts and minds of the world's English-speakers. Witness all the things they call him—not all bad.

In the name of Satan

There's a story about an old Scotswoman whose husband overheard her praying for the welfare of the Deil, or Devil. Asked for an explanation, she said: "It's as well to have friends everywhere." Maybe it's such propitiatory hedging that accounts for the expression, "give the Devil his due." Certainly he seems to have more than his share of names, nicknames, and epithets, not to mention advocates.

The basic word *Devil* was *deoful* in Old English, and it came from the Greek *diabolos,* or "slanderer"—which, while pejorative, is still a pretty wimpy root for evil personified. *Satan,* the title of choice for most Bible translators since the Middle Ages, is from the Hebrew for "adversary," a little stronger than a mere mudslinger but still not as loathsome as his reputation seems to warrant. The foulest of all is *Fiend,* from the Anglo-Saxon *feond,* which in turn came from an Old Teutonic word meaning "to hate." (Whereas *friend* developed from Anglo-Saxon *freond,* which was rooted in the Old Teutonic "to love.")

Even in adjectival form, *fiendish* conveys more evil than the other two. *Satanic* is a close second, but some senses of *devilish* have ameliorated to the point where it's possible to describe something as "devilishly good." We also apply the word to a naughty child, or imp. *Imp* in Old English meant a young plant shoot or scion of a tree. About 400 years ago, it became fashionable to refer to evil persons as "imps [or sons] of the Devil" or "imps of hell." Eventually usage dropped the provenance, the original meaning became obsolete, and *imp* came to mean a little devil or demon.

Since Satan was originally an angel who went wrong in a big way, some of the epithets retain a certain reverence, such as *the Prince of Darkness, His Satanic Majesty, the Arch Fiend, Apollyon* (the destroyer), and the deferential *Old Gentleman* used by Daniel Defoe. The Latin *lucifer,* or "light-bringer," was another name for Venus, the morning star. Through a misreading of the Bible, *Lucifer* was thought to have been Satan's name before his fall. Even less grandiose terms, such as *the Wicked One, the Evil One, the Enemy of Mankind, the Tempter,* and *the Serpent,* have historically been spelled with respectful capital letters.

Some of the appellations are fancy, or fanciful. *Beelzebub,* whose first part comes from the Phoenician deity *Baal,* was the "lord of the flies" in Hebrew. More outlandish were *Frateretto, Flibberdigibbet, Hoberdidance,* and *Tocobatto,* identified as the four devils of the Morris (i.e., Moorish) Dance in 1603 by Archbishop Samuel Harsnett in his delightfully titled *Declaration of Egregious Popish Impostures.*

The adjective *old* in the friendly, familiar sense crops up often in *Old Nick*-names, again perhaps to avoid offending a future long-term landlord. The Anglo-Saxons often referred to *se ealda,* the "old 'un," and *Old Nick* has been a favourite since the 17th century, though its origin, often speculated on, is unknown. Others in this venerable category are *Old Skipper, Old Driver, Old Gooseberry, Old Roger, Old Chap, Old Fellow, Old Lad,* and *Old Harry.* When my Scottish father made a statement of firm purpose, he often prefaced it with the feigned oath, "by the Lord Harry."

Showing somewhat less esteem are *Old Bogey, Old Botheration, Old Impostor, Old Thief,* and *Old Ruffian.* Some are redolent of fire-and-brimstone ambience, like *Old Smoke, Old Sooty, Old Blazes, Old Dragon,* and *Old Toast(er),* while others rest on imagined appearance: *Old Scratch* (though this may derive from the Old Norse *scratte* for goblin), *Old Split-foot,* and *Old Hooky* (from the pitchfork). From Robert Burns we get *Auld Hangie, Auld Hornie,* and *Auld Cloots* or *Clooty* (from Scottish *cloot* or hoof).

The deuce probably developed from the angry shout of a gambler when the "Devil's bones" turned up the despised snake-eyes. A common misconception is that *the dickens* derives from Charles Dickens, but you'd have an infernally hard time proving it, since the word appeared in Shakespeare more than 200 years before the 19th century author's birth.

It's a bit late to warn you not to read this article aloud, but you know what happens when you speak of you-know-who. I don't know why I waited so long. Maybe the Devil made me do it.

PART TWO

*

Kings, knights, and knaves

Some individuals have made heroic contributions to the English language. Others have made significant ones, consciously or unconsciously. Still others have tried—for the most part unsuccessfully—to twist our tongue in various ways.

King Alfred is best known for burning his buns through carelessness. What's much less known is why the 9th century monarch is the only "great" one in British history.

A toast to the king of English

Nineteen eighty-seven was a big year for birthdays. Air Canada, the Golden Gate Bridge, Snow White, and the jet engine turned 50. It was the centenary of celluloid film, the commercial electric lamp, Esperanto, and Sherlock Holmes's debut, in *A Study in Scarlet.* It was the 200th birthday of the U.S. Constitution, 300 for Newton's *Philosophiae Naturalis Principia Mathematica,* and 600 for Chaucer's *Canterbury Tales.*

Lost in this birthday barrage was the anniversary of an event much more significant, if more obscure, than all the others put together. It was the 1,100th anniversary of the start of a movement that had a profound effect on my ability to write this article and your ability to read it.

It took place on Martinmas Day in a chilly chamber in Edington, on the fringe of England's Salisbury Plain. Alfred, King of England (or what was left of it after five decades of Viking marauding), turned to Asser, his bishop, and said: "We must translate the books that are most needful for all men to know into the language which we can all understand, and we must teach the young men of England to read them."

So began a revival of the English language that has

grown, mostly unabated if not unassailed, to this day. Nearly two centuries later, England lost its throne to William the Conqueror, but it didn't lose its language. The language, in fact, got stronger and richer.

What Alfred began was, in the words of historian A.J. Mapp, Jr., the "greatest literary tradition in the Occident." In a populace with a literacy rate of almost zero, he kindled an interest in language and prose that eventually sparked the brilliance of Shakespeare, Milton, Wordsworth, and Dickens.

Ironically, most English school children (and probably adults) are more familiar with the legendary King Arthur, a more romantic but less substantial hero. A sophisticated level of knowledge of Alfred usually involves awareness of the apocryphal account of his burning some bannock cakes through inattention.

Literary pursuits were certainly not his main priority when he came to the throne in 871. England for the most part was overrun by Scandinavians with funny hats, funny names (there was no Hagar the Horrible, but among the invaders was one Ivarr the Boneless), and distinctly unfunny ways of striking up acquaintances.

Historians disagree on whether Alfred and his warriors chased the Viking barbarians into the north country or reached a coexistence agreement. In any event, by the late 870s, things had calmed down enough to allow Alfred to turn his attention to more cerebral matters.

To preserve the English culture, he decided, people needed to have an appreciation of English history. To achieve this, they had to be able to read, preferably in the language they spoke. Since virtually all written material was in Latin, Alfred set out to master that language. Then he personally began the task of translating all the "needful" books into English–or what we now call Old English.

This was no snap, considering the first dictionary, Robert Cawdry's *Table Alphabeticall*, was still more than 700 years in the future, and English physician Peter

Mark Roget wasn't to publish his handy thesaurus until 1852.

This was a blessing in disguise. With a limited lexicon, Alfred was forced to keep the works short and understandable. Asser, who became the king's first biographer, noted that Alfred "translates word by word infrequently. His usual practice is dissolving the long Latin sentences, dense with nouns and participles, into combinations of short clauses that may preserve little more than [the] thesis. He has culled the sense while rejecting both the complicated rhetoric and syntax that support it."

Alfred translated Pope Gregory's *Cura Pastoralis* and sent a copy to every bishop in the kingdom. He sent this and other translated works to judges, and ordered them to learn to read, have someone read for them, or resign. His fervour inspired the systematic compilation of the *Anglo-Saxon Chronicle*, an irreplaceable record of English history from the early Christian period to the 12th century.

Many English men and women, of blue blood and red, have matched or surpassed Alfred's valour in struggles to preserve English soil. But his battles to save the common language remain unparalleled.

"His unique importance in the history of English letters," wrote historian Sir Frank Stenton, "comes from his conviction that a life without knowledge or reflection was unworthy of respect, and his determination to bring the thought of the past within the range of his subjects' understanding. The translations of ancient books by which he tried to reach this end form the beginning of English prose literature."

It's for this reason that, in 11 centuries of British royalty, Alfred is the only monarch on whom posterity has bestowed that splendid sobriquet, "the Great."

James Murray's name isn't a household word. Nor are many of the half-million words in the Oxford English Dictionary, *a language monument for which he was the chief architect.*

The ultimate wordsmith

If there is a word to describe James Augustus Henry Murray, it will be found among the half-million-plus entries in the *Oxford English Dictionary.* And, unless it was coined in the past 75 years, he probably put it there.

Murray, a plodding, pertinacious Border Scot, gave 36 years of his life to editing the *OED,* possibly the greatest dictionary of any tongue and certainly one of the monumental works of the English language. But in spite of the preeminence of his work, Murray's name is not a household word–a fact that would neither surprise nor disappoint the lexicographer himself.

Murray didn't take on the daunting job for fame. His modesty was such that he actually considered declining Prime Minister Herbert Asquith's offer of a knighthood–partly because he didn't think he deserved it, and partly because he feared his favourite merchants might raise their prices in honour of his new status.

He certainly didn't do it for the money. The original contract signed with the Oxford University Press in 1878 called for a total remuneration of 6,500 pounds sterling (about $13,000 in today's money) over 10 years. This was to cover not only Murray's salary, but also those of his assistants, plus the costs of such things as postage (so prolific a user of Her Majesty's Post was Murray that a mail box was installed outside his front door), stationery, and reference books.

That hopelessly inadequate stipend would nicely cover the cost of four copies of the 20-volume second edition of the *OED,* if you were to buy them today.

Murray deserves to be better known. In addition to being a schoolteacher of consummate skill and sensitivity, he was an accomplished amateur archaeologist, geologist, mathematician, linguist, phoneticist, and scientist.

It has been suggested, only half in jest, that he was the grandfather of the telephone. One day the son of a colleague expressed an interest in electricity. Eager to impart knowledge, Murray cobbled together a crude battery from halfpennies and pieces of zinc. This contraption enthralled the youth, whose name was Alexander Graham Bell.

Murray amazingly found time for hobbies, which included gardening, tramping in the mountains, bicycling, stamp collecting, drawing, and writing. He believed these eclectic interests, all pursued with a consuming, scholarly ardour, helped prepare him for the task of compiling what turned out to be a virtual biography of the English language. Late in life he wrote that "the whole training of my life with its multifarious and irregular incursions into nearly every science and many arts, seems to have had the express purpose of fitting me to do this Dictionary."

That destiny was not always so manifest to him. Having *the* definitive English dictionary was not at the top of everybody's priority list in the second half of the 19th century. In fact, English hardly ranked as a fit subject for school study. Latin and Greek were still paramount; at Cambridge there were only two lecturers in English, and at Marlborough the English teacher had less prestige than the dancing master.

The acknowledged leading English dictionary of the day was Noah Webster's, published in 1828. What little interest there was in the cradle of the language centred on the Philological Society, whose members decided in 1858 that the world needed "a completely new English Dictionary." For 20 years they collected materials for it, but worried little about how and when it might be put together.

That was where J.A.H. Murray came in. (Murray had no given middle names. He adopted the initials "A.H." in order to have his byline distinguished from the many other James Murrays in southern Scotland; a waggish friend devised the Augustus Henry names to lend ironic pomp to the very unpompous Murray. They stuck.)

When Murray took on the editorship of the "New English Dictionary on Historical Principles," and the Oxford Delegates agreed, with something less than unanimous enthusiasm, to fund it, the guess was that it would take 10 years and that the work would take up four volumes and about 6,400 pages. But after five years, though Murray and his helpers worked like bees, they had only reached the word *ant* in the dictionary.

The "problem" was Murray's passionate (as only a devout, teetotal Scot can be) insistence on thoroughness and perfection. This dictionary would not only define every English word from the mid-12th century, it would give every subtle change in meaning and usage, and provide quotations from written works to demonstrate the evolution.

To this end, books were sent to hundreds of readers, mostly volunteers. They sent back slips of paper on which they had jotted down words in their literary contexts. These, by the millions, were stored in alphabetical pigeonholes in Murray's workshop, which he called the Scriptorium. This collection method was borrowed from that used by the brothers Grimm who, besides writing fairy tales, worked on the definitive German dictionary called the *Deutsches Woerterbuch.*

Murray had problems of his own. Poor handwriting

from many of the readers plagued the editorial staff. One paid reader gave a different cause for vexation. She claimed payment for 110 hours spent collecting 144 words, a task Murray felt should have taken no more than 12 hours. Besides that, none of her contributions was usable. Her name was Eleanor Marx, and she was the daughter of Karl Marx.

Interest at Oxford cooled further in the face of this snail's pace progress. The Delegates, who understandably wanted to see the project completed in their lifetime (they didn't), urged compromises, shortcuts, and a slackening of academic principle. There were bitter squabbles as Murray continued to exceed the agreed standard of "four times Webster" in length. The painstaking Murray resisted (in the end, the *OED* was more like eight times Webster), and on several occasions threatened to quit. But he stayed with it until his death in 1915, when the dictionary had reached the letter T.

It was finished in 1928, 70 years after its inception and 50 years after Murray signed up for a decade's work.

It's interesting that, in spite of technology, it has taken another 60 years to produce the second edition. But the Oxford people, in collaboration with the University of Waterloo, came up with a snappy encore: You can now get the *OED* on a compact computer disk. That sounds like the next best thing to bibliophile's heaven—which is probably where James Murray is holding forth right now.

Over the years, many people have wanted to reform the English language, ridding it of strange spelling, odd words, and the like. Luckily, they have all failed.

If it works, don't fix it

The readers not only write but telephone. One of the oddest calls was from a fellow who wanted to enlist me in his campaign to reform the English language, thus possibly augmenting his army by 100 per cent.

He wanted me to help him pick the language up and beat it like a dusty old carpet, ousting all the funny spellings– *-ough's, -ight's, -ould's, ph's,* etc.–and all the ambiguous homonyms and grammatical irregularities. In the end we would have a clear, simple, and permanent tongue–*with rules enforced by a commission.*

Presumably with such simplicity and sanction, one would be either literate or incarcerated. The fact that such a utilitarian language would have precluded Shakespeare and other notables didn't seem to bother him–a small price, he implied, for universal literacy and an end to such barbarisms as split infinitives and dangling participles.

This caller is not by any means the first to feel the need to "fix" English. While writers such as Chaucer and Shakespeare revelled in the linguistic anarchy of their time, later *literati*–particularly in the century and a half after 1650–developed an itch to reform, perfect, and fix the language. A contemporary synonym for fix was *ascertain* (to make certain) and it became a buzzword among the language reformers. The fact that today it means something quite different (to learn, or find out) testifies to their failure.

The fixers had several motives. This was the Age of Reason, marked by a widespread yearning for logic and rationalism after the upheavals of the Great Rebellion and the Restoration. There is no historical evidence that common people marched about with banners reading, "We Want An Immutable Language–Now!" but there was much agitation among the *learned* for certainty. Second, both Italy and France had academies to purify and safeguard their language, so why couldn't England?

The third reason had more to do, I think, with egotism than purism. Writers such as Dryden, Pope, and Swift feared that a constantly changing language would in time render their deathless prose distinctly indecipherable, as it had done to Chaucer. How can any genius, asked Swift both rhetorically and immodestly, sit down and write "with spirit and cheerfulness, when he considers that he . . . in an age or two shall hardly be understood without an interpreter?"

One of the preposterously naive things about the demands for a language tribunal was the apparent belief, on the part of otherwise brilliant people, that English speakers already possessed more words than they would ever need. In 1697 Daniel Defoe pushed for an academy "with a judicature over the learning of the age" and a power to "correct and censure the exorbitance of writers." There was no need for new words, he said, and under his tribunal "it would be as criminal then to coin words as money."

Swift was the most energetic of the fixers, and in 1712 he issued *A Proposal for Correcting, Improving, and Ascertaining the English Tongue.* It never got off the drawing board, however, because Queen Anne, who had been flirting with the idea of protecting English, died in 1714 and was succeeded by the Hanoverian George I, who couldn't speak it. Later reform attempts, including a comparatively recent stab by George Bernard Shaw, also bombed.

A voice of reason during the Age of Reason was the poet, playwright, and pamphleteer John Oldmixon, who published a 35-page attack on Swift's proposal. "The Doctor," wrote Oldmixon, "may as well set up a Society to find out the *Grand Elixir,* the *Perpetual Motion* . . . as to fix our language beyond [our] own Times."

The era saw more fruitful pursuits. Grammar pioneers such as Joseph Priestley, Robert Lowth, and Noah Webster expounded sets of "rules" for us all to break. And inspired philologues such as Samuel Johnson pinned down word spellings and meanings in practical compilations called dictionaries.

These were a quick and temporary fix, however, and the language has been blithely changing ever since—as it has also in pseudo-regulated Italy and France. Priestley (who, incidentally, discovered oxygen one day when he wasn't doing much else) wrote: "In all controversies, it is better to wait the decisions of time, which are slow and sure, than to take those of synods, which are often hasty and injudicious."

Amen. Having a "fixed" language sounds too much like being tongue-tied.

Some historical figures are remembered for dastardly deeds or high-minded heroics. Others are forgotten although their monikers are household words such as cardigan, doily, and leotard.

Names that live in eponymy

Three decades ago somebody decapitated the famous Little Mermaid in Copenhagen harbour. And two centuries ago on the same date, in Paris, a hapless highwayman called Pelletier also lost his head, an unwilling and unwitting protagonist in a drama that lives in eponymy.

The Little Mermaid got her head back. For the French felon, the severance was both permanent and precedent-setting. He was the first person to be executed by means of a new and efficient device to become known as the guillotine.

It's ironic that this macabre machine, symbol of bloodshed and terror in revolutionary France, bears the name of its designer, Dr. Joseph Ignace Guillotin. The doctor was, by all accounts, a humanitarian who was appalled at the cruel and often messy methods of dispatching delinquents–the rope for peasants and the sword for nobler necks. Moreover, the disparity in death-dealing methods was unegalitarian and therefore politically incorrect for the time.

Engineering of Guillotin's design was left to Dr. Antoine Louis, and for a while the instrument was known as "la Louisette," echoing the names of both the technician and the ruling Louis XVI. But *guillotine* caught on, and both the machine and the name were used in France until 1977.

It is the way with eponymous words that the eponym (the person after whom something is named; from Greek *epi,* upon, and *onyma,* name) has little or no say in the common words that derive from his or her handle. Some are felicitous, such as the array of flowers named for their discoverers. Some recognize a scientific or technological achievement (braille, ampere, diesel, daguerre, pasteurize). Some are immortalized in words for everyday items (cardigan, chesterfield, doily, leotard, sandwich). And others have become synonymous, deservedly or not, with various forms of villainy or absurdity.

Gen. Jean Martinet built Europe's first modern army under Louis XIV, with a system of precise and unsparing drill. Needless to say, he won no popularity polls among the ranks, and he was killed by "friendly fire" at the siege of Duisburg in 1672. His name lives on as a term for a ruthless disciplinarian.

Nicholas Chauvin, a soldier in the First Republic, probably didn't mind *martinets.* So enthusiastic was he about his country that, after being severely mutilated in battle, he still sang the praises of France and Napoleon. He became well known, but real fame arrived when a play, featuring a character based on Chauvin, became popular during the 1830s. From then on, *chauvinism* denoted exaggerated national pride, and later still, excessive belief in the superiority of one's class or cause.

Time has been kinder to Étienne de Silhouette. The 18th century controller-general became the most unpopular man in all Gaul by tripling the head tax on bachelors, making elected officials pay taxes, slapping a sales tax on all goods, reducing pensions of the nobility, and even slashing the royal household budget. A style of pocketless trousers became known derisively as *à la Silhouette,* but it was not these that carried his name forward, but his harmless hobby of cutting profiles out of black paper.

Goodman Derrick also escaped becoming one of history's bad men. Around 1600, he was the hangman at

Tyburn, the notorious London execution site, and is credited with more than 3,000 state killings. His name became a synonym for the gallows, and later for any large gibbetlike structure used for lifting. Only the latter meaning remains.

A Scottish borderer called John Duns was not so lucky. He became one of the greatest British philosophers of the Middle Ages, and attracted a large group of disciples known as Dunsmen or Dunses. After Duns's death, his followers persisted in his intricate, hair-splitting teachings, and became discredited during the Renaissance. The word *dunce* derives from the ridicule they received.

Ambrose ("Amby") Philips would probably have preferred other eponymous *éclat.* The early 18th century English poet at first won acclaim from contemporaries and critics. His reputation plummeted when he began penning insipid verses for children of the well-heeled, including such lines as "dimpled damsel, sweetly smiling." Coined in his honour was an adjective that fittingly rhymes with his nickname, *namby-pamby.*

And little did Juliet know that Romeo–whose name would otherwise "smell as sweet"–would become a word for a man's house slipper.

William Cobbett, alias Peter Porcupine, was a colourful champion of the English language. He was born in a pub and became an irascible social and political commentator.

An outrageous man of the quill

A passing reference I made some time ago to one William Cobbett brought this response from a reader in Edmonton: "Your mention of that . . . worthy gent means I now know of three persons living who have heard of him."

Heard of him! He's one of my heroes. Cobbett is certainly no household name. Yet, in the late 18th century and early 19th, there were probably few Englishmen or Americans who didn't accord the name instant recognition–and who didn't either revere him or hate him.

Cobbett was best-known in his time as a prickly political journalist. In England, he defended traditional rural values against the juggernaut of the Industrial Revolution and rampant corruption in the public service. During two sojourns in the U.S., he ruffled feathers with his waspish antirepublicanism, and earned the nickname "Peter Porcupine"–which he eagerly adopted as a pseudonym.

Much less celebrated is that Cobbett was possibly the most passionate, polemical, prejudiced, and perfectly outrageous champion the English language ever had.

Born in a Surrey pub called the Jolly Farmer, the later abstemious Cobbett did a stint with a London law firm, where he formed the typically hasty opinion that a knowledge of grammar was the key to success in any endeavour. He joined the army at age 21, and while waiting for an overseas posting, he whiled away guard duty by memorizing and reciting, in its entirety, Robert Lowth's *A Short Introduction to English Grammar* (1762).

The posting was to New Brunswick, where he spent seven years alienating most of his fellow soldiers and infuriating all of his superiors. He endured, however, because he did all of the regiment's important work. As he explained it, with characteristic immodesty:

> My path was full of rocks and pit-falls; and as I never disguised my dislikes or restrained my tongue, I should have been broken and flogged for 50 different offenses, given to my superior jack-asses, had they not been kept in awe by my inflexible sobriety, by the consciousness of their inferiority to me, and by the real and almost indispensable necessity of the use of my talents.

Back in England in 1791, he tried to have his officers court-martialled for corruption, only to find he was taking on the entire British system of government. He fled to revolutionary France, then to the U.S., where his career as an irascible social and political commentator blossomed. After a costly libel action he returned to England, where his "splendid scurrility" (as G.K. Chesterton put it) found full flower in his newspaper, the *Political Register.* He served a two-year jail term for denouncing the flogging of disgruntled militiamen, and in 1817 returned to the U.S. to avoid further run-ins with British authority.

At a Long Island farm, he decided to share his language wisdom with the world. Letters originally written to his son, James, were published in 1823 as *A Grammar of the English Language,* with the subtitle, *Intended for the Use of Schools and of Young Persons in general; but*

more especially for the Use of Soldiers, Sailors, Apprentices, and Plough-Boys. TO WHICH ARE ADDED, ***Six Lessons, intended to prevent Statesmen from using false grammar, and from writing in an awkward manner.***

False grammar he found everywhere, but took particular delight in exposing it in such luminaries as Samuel Johnson, the Duke of Wellington, and university fellows "who live by the sweat of other people's brows." Of Lord Castlereagh he wrote: "What do you say, what can you say, of such a man, but that nature might have made him for a valet, for a strolling player, and possibly for an auctioneer; but never for a Secretary of State. Yet this man was *educated* at the *University of Cambridge*" (Cobbett's italics).

The bristly text does squeeze some solid, early 19th century grammar lessons in between the vitriolic volleys. Also some common sense: "The bad writing, on which I am about to remark, I do not pretend to look on as the cause of the present public calamities . . . but, it is a proof of a deficiency in that sort of talent which appears to me to be necessary in men entrusted with great affairs. He who writes badly thinks badly."

More on Peter Porcupine coming up.

William Cobbett disliked overuse of superlatives. But the quixotic author drew extreme reactions with his uncompromising invective against the Establishment.

An incisive wielder of the verbal knife

If you had been browsing in a bookshop around 1825, you might have seen an advertisement for *A Grammar of the English Language,* by William Cobbett. Penned by the author himself, this was no ordinary publisher's puffery. It stated, matter-of-damned-factly, that the book had a printing of 55,000 copies–a best-seller in those days–"without ever having been mentioned by the old shuffling bribed sots, called Reviewers."

That gives you just a little taste of the horny-fisted, hang-the-rascals rhetorical style of this quirky, quixotic writer, whom author G.K. Chesterton later labelled "the noblest English example of the noble calling of the agitator."

William Cobbett's name would not be a shoo-in for anyone's list of the all-time greatest English writers. Nor would his prickly pen-name, Peter Porcupine. Yet early last century he was renowned, and, depending on which side of the Industrial Revolution (or the Atlantic Ocean) you were on, he was either an idol or anathema.

Cobbett's notoriety didn't spring from his preachings on grammar and language usage. His weekly newspaper, the *Political Register,* was the principal wheel on which he ground his axe. And you dared not miss an issue of it, whether he was your pet or your *bête noire.*

Uncompromising invective against the Establishment—church, government, military, judiciary, academia—also bristled within the covers of such innocuously titled books as *Cottage Economy* (1822), *The English Gardener* (1829), and his best known work, *Rural Rides* (1830). His writings had a common theme: They aimed, through practical advice or contemptuous examples, to improve the lot of working families, whom he considered the ravaged victims of industrialization, incompetence, and epidemic inhumanity.

Knowledge to combat these evils existed in books, he believed, and grammar was the "gate entrance" to all paths of knowledge.

Cobbett's *Grammar* is unlike any other grammar text you'll ever read. Because it comprises letters originally written to his son, James, the instruction is all in the second person, creating for the reader the arresting sense of a personal tutorial.

Many of the grammatical conventions are dated, but the principles are as fresh as this morning. He urges James to remember "that the *only* use of words is to *cause our meaning to be clearly understood,* and that the best words are those, which are familiar to the ears of the greatest number of people."

What truly sets this grammar apart is its entertaining mixture of pedagogy and polemics. Cobbett doesn't pass up a chance to twist the knife. To illustrate how some nouns may be collective, or nouns of multitude, he pointedly mingles these examples: "*Mob, Parliament, Rabble, House of Commons, Regiment, Court of King's Bench, Den of Thieves.*"

He rails against mealy mouthed adjectives. "Amongst a select society of empty heads, 'moderate reform' has long been a fashionable expression," he says, then wonders rhetorically how those nitwits "would like to obtain *moderate justice* in a court of law, or to meet with *moderate chastity* in a wife." And what could you expect from statesmen whose solution to unemployment was to assign "labourers to dig holes one day and fill them up the next"?

Men of letters were not spared. Milton, Johnson, Hume, Addison, and Goldsmith were all targets for Cobbett's needles. His favourite pin-cushion was Secretary of State Lord Castlereagh, who slit his own throat two months after Cobbett's last attack on him. Comparing Castlereagh and the Duke of Wellington, he wrote: "There is, in the nonsense of Castlereagh, a frivolity and foppery that give it a sort of liveliness, and that now-and-then elicit a smile," but with the Iron Duke, "there is nothing to relieve: all is vulgar, all clumsy, all dull, all torpid inanity."

Cobbett may have anticipated the excesses of 20th century hucksterism when he wrote: "Weak minds, feeble writers and speakers, delight in *superlatives.* They have big sound in them, and give the appearance of *force;* but they very often betray those who use them into absurdities."

Cobbett's salvoes were low on syllables and high on impact. As Chesterton put it: "Conventional writers use heavy words so lightly; and he used light words so heavily; every homely word like a hatchet."

Cobbett's *Grammar* is, unfortunately, out of print. With luck, you may find a 1984 Oxford reissue at your library.

The Bowdlers did their best to keep the English language clean. They produced a Family Shakespeare *that excised everything that could "raise a blush on the cheek of modesty."*

*

Ot—o and other classical Bowdlerdash

It was a d—d disgrace! There it was, Thomas Bowdler's bl—dy birthday, and as far as I could tell, there wasn't so much as a tea party at the Women's Christian Temperance Union to honour the old son-of-a-bleep. So, we just had to settle for a few words, if not well-chosen, certainly well-scrubbed.

Dr. Bowdler was the eponym for the verb *bowdlerize,* which means to expurgate writing by omitting or changing "improper" words or phrases. In his time, the common word for such activity was "castrating," which, curiously, was not considered offensive.

Bowdler was born on July 11, 1754, presumably about nine months after an unspeakable–certainly unmentionable–act on the part of Thomas and Elizabeth Bowdler. During a childhood unedified by such classics as *Teenage Mutant Ninja Turtles,* the *Simpsons,* or even *Leave It To B—r,* young Thomas had to make do with sonorous and straitlaced readings by Squire Bowdler of *Hamlet, Ot—o,* and *T—us Andronicus*–but probably not *Romeo and Juliet* or *The R—e of Lucrece.*

Later, Dr. Bowdler realized his father had shielded him and his siblings from the coarser passages, by leaving them out or skilfully rewording them. The pious and precious Victorian art of bowdlerization had begun–long before the word was coined, and seven decades before the 18-year-old Victoria hitched up her petticoat (sorry about that) and climbed on the throne.

True bowdlerization got under way in 1807, with the anonymous publication in Bath of the four-volume *Family Shakespeare.* According to the preface, everything was excised "that can raise a blush on the cheek of modesty." This turned out to be a whopping one-tenth of the Bard's words–including such indelicacies as "belly" and "grunt," and any other words that might kindle unwarranted passion, such as "thigh."

Suspicions that the author was Bowdler–who retired as a physician at age 31 because he couldn't stand sick people–were confirmed when his name appeared as editor in a new, 1818 edition. A century later it became clear that the original bowdlerizer was not Thomas, but his sister Harriet. She, a 50-year-old spinster, had to remain anonymous, of course, or admit that she was familiar enough with filth to know what to cut or euphemize.

The rise and fall of bowdlerism, and its modern rebirth under the banner of political rectitude, are wittily recounted in a recent, revised edition of Noel Perrin's *Dr. Bowdler's Legacy* (Nonpareil Books, 1992). Professor Perrin, who teaches at Dartmouth College, credits or blames four major developments for the original phenomenon. Eighteenth century Britain was a cold-bed of propriety and sensibility, nurtured by the growing conviction that the Union had reached the summit of civilization. A second was the Industrial Revolution and the emergence of "commuter husbands." A third was the rise of evangelical religion, particularly Methodism.

Perhaps most important was the development of cheap paper and the expansion of the reading public. "It is probably a general truth," writes Professor Perrin, "that the larger the audience, whether for television, books, or cheese spreads, the blander the fare. There are more prejudices to avoid offending."

In the event, the urge to purge burgeoned, and no author of any repute escaped the blue-stockinged blue-pencillers. At its peak, says Professor Perrin, some prudes even felt it necessary to keep male and female authors separate on 19th century bookshelves. In the Victorian order of curses, Lady Macbeth got her wish: the "damned spot" was out.

Dictionaries were another principal target, and here Noah Webster was the great white-washer. But the toughest challenge to the expurgators was the Bible, which, as everyone knows, is chock-full of harlotry, adultery, sodomy, onanism–as well as stories that, as one Biblical bowdlerizer said, could "only tend to excite ideas the worse calculated for a female breast."

Bad words in the Good Book brought about the verb that immortalizes the dour doctor's name. British MP Perronet Thompson, in an 1836 letter to his constituents, noted that there were certain names in the gospel that ultra-Christians "would probably have Bowdlerized."

Professor Perrin's new book has a chapter called "The Current Scene." I won't give away the ending, but the author is confident today's race-based bowdlerism will pass in time. Personally, I wouldn't sw—r to it.

By invention, by popularizing Scottish dialect, and by reviving long-dormant English words, the author of the epic best-seller Ivanhoe *made major contributions to our language.*

The awesome legacy of Sir Walter Scott

If you were alive and literate in the early 19th century English-speaking world, you would almost certainly have read, or be reading, *Ivanhoe,* the epic best-seller by Sir Walter Scott. In it you would have encountered the unfamiliar term *free lance* in a passage describing Sir Maurice de Bracy's company of mercenaries.

The term would have been strange to you and contemporary readers because Scott invented it. And because he was the most popular writer of his day, *free lance* gained wide circulation. Though in *Ivanhoe* it had the archaic smack of chivalry and derring-do, it soon gained new figurative meanings.

One of these was *free-lance journalist,* a "mercenary" member of the fourth estate who has Sir Walter Scott to thank for this romantic label–certainly an improvement over the pre-Scott sobriquet, "penny-a-liner."

Free-lance is one of many modern English terms for which all of us are in Scott's debt. By invention, by popularizing Scottish dialect, and by reviving long dormant English words, Scott's contributions to our language are considered by many to be second in importance only to those of Shakespeare.

Long before Scott became a prolific writer he was a voracious reader. And he possessed a memory bordering on awesome–a word that was familiar to Scott's countrymen, but virtually unknown to other English speakers until it appeared in *Rob Roy* in 1817. It's now suffering somewhat from overfamiliarity.

Scott devoured literature, particularly Elizabethan and Jacobean writings, and Border ballads and stories. To this voracity we owe *henchman*. From the Old English *hengest*, horse, this word originally meant a stable groom. The last citation in the *Oxford English Dictionary* for this sense is from Sir Walter Ralegh's *Remains* in 1618. It reappeared as *hanchman* more than a century later when a Highlander named Edward Burt, in *Letters from a Gentleman in the North of Scotland,* recorded it as "a sort of secretary" who was prepared "to venture his life in defence of his master; and at drinking-bouts he stands behind his seat, at his haunch . . . "

When Scott stumbled on the latter, he stored it for use in *Waverly,* where it describes Fergus McIvor's "right-hand man" (and where Scott repeated, in a note, Burt's etymologically dubious definition), giving the archaic word new life. The shady senses of political hatchet-man or goon were later U.S. adaptations.

Such a right-hand man might be caught *red-handed,* but not before *Ivanhoe,* where Sir Reginald Front-de-Boeuf first uttered the adjective. Scott adapted it from an old Scottish law that referred to murderers being arrested "with the red hand."

One of the first scholars to recognize Scott's endowment to English was Ernest Weekley, a classics professor at University College, Nottingham. In an essay in the *Atlantic Monthly* in 1931, Professor Weekley said Shakespeare's unparalleled legacy of colourful words and phrases would have been somewhat diminished if Walter Scott had not salvaged some of them from the scrap-heap of obsolescence.

Shakespeare used the word *fitful* only once, in *Macbeth.* This expressive word next saw the light of day in Scott's *Lady of the Lake,* 205 years later, to describe a capricious breeze. *Hamlet* spoke of a *towering passion* and *yeoman's service.* The first resurfaced 216 years later in *Rob Roy,* and Scott not only borrowed the Bard's *yeoman's service,* but also reached back more than four centuries to resurrect Chaucer's adverb *yeomanly.*

Scott nourished English from the larder of Scottish border dialects. He gave us *blackmail,* an early protection racket in which free-lance highland tax collectors bled lowland farmers. All Scots have been *canny* since *The Antiquary,* and the sturdy word *stalwart* slept for more than two centuries before Scott rallied it to new service. Then there are *slogan, smouldering, raid, uncanny, weird, bluff, daft, gruesome,* and *glamour,* which were not only "as old as the hills" (*The Monastery*) but nearly as dead as doornails when Scott rescued them.

Sad to say, he was less successful with other inventions. Somehow, I'd rather tell my troubles to a *bleed-barrel* than a bartender, even though he might consider me a hopeless *swill-flagon.*

Sir Walter Scott revived, popularized, or invented scores of words that are still in common usage today. Perhaps that's why the great man's novels smoulder with such gruesome glamour.

*

An uncanny verbal benefactor

The year was 1808. Sir Walter Scott's sweeping narrative poem *Marmion: A Tale of Flodden Field* was hot off the press, but got a lukewarm reception in his home town. "His genius, seconded by the omnipotence of fashion, has brought chivalry again into temporary favour," wrote critic Francis Jeffrey in the *Edinburgh Review.* "Fine ladies and gentlemen now talk indeed of donjons, keeps, tabards, scutcheons . . . portcullises, wimples, and we know not what besides."

This was a peevish way of admitting that Scott had a profound influence on the early 19th century reading public. What Jeffrey couldn't know is that the Edinburgh lawyer/poet/novelist's influence would continue for nearly two centuries more–and that long after the tabards were tucked back into fashion's closet, other words that Scott invented, revived, or popularized would become part of the common language.

Earlier we looked at a few Scott coinages and revivals, and briefly mentioned a few others. They're worth a closer peek.

Gruesome, from the Scottish verb *grue,* to shudder from terror, appeared in *Old Mortality,* published in

1816–"He's as grave and gruesome an auld Dutchman as e'er I saw." Before any partisans point out that Robert Burns used it 40 years earlier, it should be recorded that Scott outsold Burns (outside Scotland) by about 100 to 1. It was, beyond doubt, Scott who popularized the word.

Dr. Samuel Johnson was mystified when he entered *smouldering* in his 1755 dictionary: "This word seems a participle, but I know not whether the verb *smoulder* be in use." It wasn't. The participial adjective was still being used by poets such as Milton and Dryden, but the verb was an all-but-dead ember during the 17th and 18th centuries. In 1805, Scott's *Lady of the Lake* referred to the feud which "smoulders in Roderick's breast," thus giving the obsolescent word a new life and a new glamour.

That beguiling word *glamour* is a corruption of *grammar*. It first meant magic or enchantment, a reflection of the average medieval person's distrust of book-learning (the only grammar studied at the time was Latin, which was all Greek to the hoi polloi). Burns used *glamour* as witchcraft in *Capt. Grose's Peregrin* in 1789. But again, it was Scott, a quarter-century later, who gave the word broad currency by using it in *Lay of the Last Minstrel*–a work that, according to philologist Ernest Weekley, enjoyed an acclaim "which is now attained only by the lucky thriller or pornographic novel."

Scott used the adjective *canny* (knowing, wary, frugal, cunning, formed on the verb *can*) so often that it became the indispensable modifier for Scotsmen. *Uncanny,* in the sense of weird or supernatural, was unleashed on the reading public in *Guy Mannering* (1815) when Dandie Dinmont said of Meg Merrilies, "I wish she binna uncanny! Her words dinna seem to come in God's name, or like other folk's." Scott influenced even the canine world; the Dandie Dinmont terrier is the only breed named after a fictional character.

The Old English *gedæfte* (meek, humble) gave way

in Middle English to *daffte,* and was often applied to beasts and humans in the sense of stupid, foolish, or even insane. The word *silly* had a similar evolution, beginning with the Old English *sælig,* or blessed. By the 17th century, *daffte* dwindled to *daft,* then dropped from use entirely. Scott's *Old Mortality* gave new life to this one too, with the sentence, "The woman would drive any reasonable being daft."

Our modern sense of *road* dates only from the 16th century, when it began to supplant the much older *way.* Before that, *road* (from Old English *rad,* past tense of *ridan,* to ride) meant a horseback ride. Depending on context, it could also mean a hostile incursion by mounted attackers, or an *inroad.* The Scottish version of *road* was *raid,* a word virtually unknown in England until Walter Scott used it in *Last Minstrel.* The Walter Scott-ish version of the older, more romantic sense has endured, while the English *road* has been relegated to the pedestrian (and vehicular) sense it now has.

Professor Weekley judged that, next to Shakespeare, "Scott has been our greatest verbal benefactor." Certainly great enough to ensure that he will never be, like the wretch in *Last Minstrel,* "unwept, unhonoured and unsung."

PART THREE

*

The way we word

English has many idiosyncrasies—words that are spelled alike but have opposite meanings, words that look alike but are treacherously different, words that are shrouded by myth, and words that we hardly ever use except in unusual circumstances.

If brevity is the soul of wit, it is also the heart and soul of headline writing. But many of the short words so beloved of newspaper editors are hardly ever used in everyday English.

Language shock horror

When I saw the headline "More Sandbagging" in the *Tilbury Times,* I naturally assumed that a local politician or bureaucrat had just provided another example of creative procrastination. Reading the story, I was jolted to find that the headline meant exactly what it said: Local waterfront homeowners once more had to resort to sandbags to defend their properties from the ravages of a swollen Lake Erie.

That got me thinking about how accustomed we've become to taking headlines with a metaphoric grain of salt. We're forced to, of course. Pick up any newspaper and chances are you'll find at least one headline containing a word such as cut, attack, assail, hack, slash, lash, blast, rap, rip, knock, slam, or flay. If the accompanying stories always involved the literal use of these verbs, we'd be living in a much more violent society than we dare to think. But the stories are seldom as fierce as these explosive, lacerating headline words suggest.

If brevity is the soul of wit, as Polonius said to Gertrude, it is also the heart of headline writing. This puts a unique squeeze on the headline writer, who must not only deal with the same inexorable deadlines other journalists do, but must at the same time do battle with the implacable Character Count.

The headline writer faces a third pressure. He or she is constantly being rapped, assailed, and blasted by readers, reporters, and senior editors alike for missing the point of a story. The accusations often have merit. A Toronto tabloid recently ran the heading:

Parole
for wife
killer
irks dad

Aside from the ambiguity caused by the distribution of the words in four decks, that short verb—"irks"—fell somewhat short of the mark. The first paragraph of the story said the father of the woman who was murdered by her husband was "outraged." But *outrages* wouldn't have fit. Nor would *angers, embitters, enrages, incenses,* or *ticks off. Irks* may not have been fitting, but it fit.

One of the cardinal rules of communication is to avoid jargon, yet headline writing has developed its own distinctive idiom. Many words appear in headlines that are hardly ever encountered in any other written or spoken communication, simply because they're short. A three- or four-letter word that will serve instead of a longer one is the headline-writer's ace card. This has created some classics.

An example is "thug." Borrowed from the Hindi word for a member of an Indian sect who robbed and murdered in the name of Kali, goddess of destruction, the word still lurks in headlines as a synonym for robber, mugger, hoodlum, gangster, or goon.

Some become not only classics, but classic clichés. Where else but in a headline do you read of *pacts* being *inked,* or *fêtes* being *marred?* These "short-counts" are part of a reliable stable of old standards that get the headline writer through the day. Here's a sampling:

Probe - It's difficult to find a single issue of any daily newspaper that doesn't contain this word. Real people talk of investigations, inquiries, royal commissions, hearings, inspections, reviews, studies, surveys, research, and even witch-hunts or fishing expeditions. Only headline writers and hospital operating-room staff speak of probes.

Veto - This old favourite, a steal from the first-person singular of the Latin *vetare* (to forbid) is regularly used to mean turn down, reject, give thumbs down to, disagree with, prohibit, rule out, disallow, refuse, prevent, or simply not stand for. This versatile verb is sometimes used even in its real sense–that is, to denote a disapproval with a great deal of formal authority, such as its constitutional meaning in the U.S. "Spurn" is often used as an imprecise synonym for "reject" even when the rejection does not carry the haughty Victorian disdain that spurn connotes.

Idle - Only in headlines does this adjective take on a transitive verb form. And it often cuts two ways in labour-management matters. In one situation ("Strike idles GM"), management is the recipient of the action. In another ("GM layoff idles 300 at Oshawa plant"), the workers become the object. Despite the automotive implication, idlings are not confined to the car industry.

Quash - Rumours are quashed, instead of scotched or denied. Often bids are quashed, as in a corporate takeover attempt. Lower court judgments or convictions are (erroneously) quashed. Rebellions and uprisings are seldom quashed (a correct use of the word). Nor are they quelled (also correct). Fires are quelled, when they should be quenched.

Perish - When was the last time you uttered the word perish? It's a headline habitué, and also often appears in photo captions (another subject). It usually involves large numbers of fatalities, such as in airliner crashes, volcano eruptions, earthquakes, and avalanches. But it can safely be tagged onto smaller numbers, especially if the mishap occurs at sea.

Slay - This is a nonword in modern oral English, but a common one in newspaper headlines. The past participle is its most frequent form ("Slain mountie buried"), but it is also rendered as a noun ("Police hunt slayer") and present participle ("Clues Sought [see Seek] in slaying").

Seek - No one really says seek, or its past tense, sought. They usually say looking for, or trying to get, or applying for. But in headlines, police seek killers, and solutions are sought. Often, the act of seeking, or applying for, or simply attempting to get, is referred to as a "bid." And, as we have seen, bids are often quashed, spurned, or vetoed before a pact can be inked, thereby quashing somebody's plans.

See - This one's a real workhorse, although it's seldom put to its real use in the sense of perceiving visually. It can mean predict ("Economist sees economic upturn"), consider to be, characterize as, or describe ("Canadians seen as lazy by Japanese"). A blood relative of . . .

Said - . . . as in "Canadians said apathetic," or "India said set to reject Canadian pipeline bid."

Yule - I often think this Christmas substitute was invented by a headline writer (it wasn't; it's Old English for a heathen celebration of the winter solstice). In spite of its happy association, it's often accompanied by the adjective "bleak," as in "GM idles 5,000, bleak Yule seen."

A skilled reader will be able to calculate that the average length of these "head-words" is four. There are many others–not counting the ones you'd hear if you dropped in to a newsroom about four minutes before deadline.

What is the most used word in the history of the world? We'll give you a clue. It's English, short, and isn't contained in the phrase "constitutional reform proposals."

You say goodbye and I say . . .

Hello.

You have reached WORD PLAY. We're sorry, we can't take your call right now, but please stay on the line and a columnist will be with you as soon as possible. Meanwhile, you may be interested to know that by starting this message with that little word "hello" we have helped maintain its status as the most-used word in the history of the world.

That *hello* holds this record is the plausible contention of Charles Berlitz, linguist and author of *Native Tongues,* a 340-page volume that lives up to its dust-jacket blurb as "a book of captivating language facts."

Berlitz, who is no longer connected with the language schools, says there are several reasons for *hello*'s ubiquity. One is that English is the most-spoken language on earth (besides claiming an estimated 300 million native speakers, it is by far the most popular second language), and that is how English speakers greet each other. The use of telephones–with or without tape recording appendages–and the custom in many non-English language countries to answer the phone with a variation such as *(h)allo,* have simply solidified the word's position as the number one, all-time record-holder among human utterances.

Hello was not part of the telephone-answering ritual from the beginning. According to Berlitz, the first telephone operators, in Connecticut, greeted callers with a jaunty "ahoy." For reasons not difficult to divine, especially if you live in Kansas or Saskatchewan, this salty salutation didn't catch on. In fact by the late 1890s, only a decade after Bell's infernal contraption went into commercial use, *hello* was in such common use that operators were known as "hello-girls."

But *hello* doesn't enjoy global hegemony.

In India, where English use is one of the more persistent souvenirs of colonial days, *hello* is still prevalent, but the Hindi greeting *hanji* ("greetings") is gaining ground.

In Greece a common telephone salutation is *embros* ("come in"), even though the phone ring does not sound like a knock on the door. In Italy, you're likely to be greeted with *pronto,* which means "ready" or, more loosely, "go ahead, it's your lira."

Spanish speakers have a *pronto* too. But they don't use it to answer phone calls because it means "soon," which might leave callers a bit bewildered. Instead, they have a range of openers: *con quién?* ("with whom?"), *quién habla?* ("who's speaking?"), *oigo* ("I'm listening"), and the rather contemplative *a ver* ("let's see"). Another common greeting in Spain is *digame* ("tell me"), and your call in Mexico is likely to be answered with *bueno?,* which is Spanish for "well" but is rendered more along the lines of the slightly impatient "well???"

In Russia *hallo* is popular, but for variety a phone answerer might say *shloosayu,* which translates into "I am listening," and often results in a rather moist mouthpiece. Typical Japanese graciousness is reflected in the way people answer the phone in that country, *moshi moshi* ("excuse, excuse"), whereas in China you're apt to be greeted with *wei,* a word with which the Chinese also summon farm animals to be fed.

In Swahili, the Arabic-based *lingua franca* of much of sub-Saharan Africa (where more than 700 other separate tongues exist), phones are answered with *jambo.* This means, approximately, "nothing the matter" or "all's well," as if the caller might routinely need such reassurance.

No one has ever been quite sure of the spelling of *hello.* It has been set down variously as *hallo, halloa, halloo, hullo, hulloa, hollo,* and *hillo,* not to mention all the non-English variations without the aspirated beginning. The *hello* spelling seems to be standard on this continent, while the *Oxford English Dictionary* describes it as a variant of *hallo,* under which spelling is the main entry.

According to Oxford, *hallo/hello* derives from the Old High German *halâ,* which, for the more technically minded, was the emphatic imperative mood of the verb *halôn,* or "fetch." The imperative might have been used, for example, to summon a ferryman from the other side of a river. The possible response of a ferryman to this somewhat haughty behest is not hinted at.

Hello has one other modern English meaning, as an interjection expressing discovery or a moderate degree of surprise. This very specialized usage is confined almost exclusively to English police constables who, according to standard operating procedures when happening upon a crime in progress, must declare, "Hello, what's this, then?"

Thank you for calling WORD PLAY. If you would like a discourse on the word "goodbye" please press 1; if you would like the latest sports and weather . . .

A U.S. professor has recently been getting a lot of attention because of his claim that Thomas Edison invented the word "hello." Well, the sooner we say goodbye to that notion, the better.

This "hello" theory is a wrong number

It stands to reason that the editor of an obscure and highly specialized newsletter devoted to antique phonographs would be a fairly fervent fan of Thomas Alva Edison. The record player was, after all, among the few important things the American genius dreamed up all by himself, instead of improving on other people's brain waves.

Nor should it raise any eyebrows when the same newsletter carries a fanciful yarn about how the Wizard of Menlo Park "invented" the word *hello.* But when this comical canard is given credence by *The New York Times,* by CBC-Radio's *As It Happens,* and–the ultimate cachet of credibility–by an item in the Social Studies column of *The Globe and Mail's* Facts and Arguments page, the joke has gone too far.

I'm assuming it's a joke, because the editor of the *Antique Phonograph Monthly,* Allen Koenigsberg, is also a classics professor and teaches a course in the history of English at Brooklyn College. He should know something about how words evolve. So it must be charitably assumed that he had his tongue firmly planted in his cheek when he wrote that Edison coined the little word of greeting that is now used around the world.

Professor Koenigsberg points out that the earliest citation for *hello* in the *Oxford English Dictionary* is dated 1883. But he found an earlier use in the archives of the American Telephone and Telegraph Co. in Manhattan. Dated August 15, 1877, it was a letter from Edison to T.B.A. David, a Pittsburgh businessman who was about to introduce the telephone there. It read, in part:

> *Friend David,*
> *I do not think we shall need a call bell as Hello! can be heard 10 to 20 feet away. What you think?* [sic]

This was a year and a half after the U.S. Patent Office approved patent No. 174,465 describing "the method of, and apparatus for, transmitting vocal or other sounds telegraphically . . . by causing electric undulations, similar in form to the vibrations of the air accompanying the said vocal or other sounds." But the patent for this revolutionary device, the "speaking telegraph," was not among the 1,093 granted to Thomas Edison during his life. It went instead to a rival, a young immigrant professor at Boston University, who styled himself A. Graham Bell.

Professor Koenigsberg deduces that the "Friend David" memo was "the first use of the word 'Hello' in the English language"–a leap of logic that would have made Evel Knievel envious. Rather than establishing the first use, the letter strongly suggests that both Edison and David were already familiar with *hello.* If it had never before been uttered, Edison's vaunted ego would have compelled him to make a bigger thing of his coinage. In fact, only a month before, Edison was noisily hallooing into the diaphragm of a crude contraption that would prove to be the prototype for the phonograph.

A slightly deeper delve into Oxford reveals that the word existed for more than three centuries before Edison's "invention." *Hello* is merely the latest in a long series of spelling variants for the same word, including *hallo, halloo, halloa, hullo, hulloo, hulloa, hollo,* and *hollow.*

The professor does acknowledge the earlier versions, but says they weren't greetings, but rather attention-getting shouts or exclamations of surprise.

In the early, imperfect stage of telephone technology, people invariably raised their voices when using the contraption–the way some people still unnecessarily do when talking long distance. The sense and use of the word as a hailed greeting are identical to those conveyed in a passage from *The Pleasant History of the Two Angry Women of Abington,* written by Henry Porter in 1599: "Why, hollow to me, and I will answer thee."

It may well be true that Edison popularized the word. Being both hearing-impaired and spelling-disadvantaged, he may also be responsible for the modern spelling. But to say he invented *hello* is carrying invention too far. Maybe next we'll hear that Archimedes invented *Eureka!*

Government budgets can be baffling as well as impoverishing. Let's take a look at the origins of some of the words that are bandied about when times get taxing.

Tracing our fiscal forebears

Albert Einstein was reputedly no slouch at putting two and two together, or, for that matter, taking them apart. There was one numbers game, however, that baffled him. "The hardest thing in the world to understand," he said, "is income tax."

This is not going to be a primer for the fiscally flummoxed. However, when budgets loom on federal and provincial horizons, it might be well to understand the origins of some of the terminology.

The word *budget* is from the French *bougette,* meaning a little pouch, wallet, or purse, usually made of leather. It carried this meaning in English from the 14th to the late 19th century, and during that time, "to open your budget" was a metaphor for speaking your mind.

The little purse metaphorically became a big one some time in the 17th century, when *budget* began to be used to describe the annual statement of expected revenue and expenditure read to the British House of Commons by the Chancellor of the Exchequer. *Exchequer,* from the Latin for chessboard, reflects the early practice of kings and their money men of totting up their tithes and other tribute on a large tablecloth divided into squares.

Budgets and their authors have never ranked high in popularity polls. According to one of the quirky little notes the *OED* appends to some entries, a 1733 pamphlet compared Sir Robert Walpole to a "mountebank opening his wallet of quack medicines and conjuring tricks." In fact, for over 200 years until the early 19th century, a *budgeter* was a strolling player, and often a charlatan.

It's hard to resist mentioning that *budget* is related etymologically to *belly* (in Old English *bælg* for bag, skin, envelope), *bellows, bulge,* and *bilge* (the belly or bulging part of a ship; in Modern English, balderdash).

The Latin *fiscus,* for rush-basket or purse, was adapted in English as *fisc* or *fisk* to denote the privy purse of the Roman Emperor. By generalization it came to mean any royal or state treasury, but fell into disuse in the last century. The adjective *fiscal* has survived to describe things financial, usually those matters falling within a 12-month period, the normal life expectancy of a budget.

It should come as no surprise to taxpayers that another descendant of the same word ancestor is *confiscate,* which originally meant to appropriate private property to the royal or public treasury, and has come to mean any forcible or authoritarian seizure. Another old word for confiscate was *escheat,* which for some reason has given us our modern word *cheat.*

About 900 years ago, the medieval words *taske* and *taxe,* from the Latin *taxere* (to appraise or censure) meant the same thing–to rate, assess, levy, reckon. The former evolved into a work sense, albeit work usually imposed as a duty, while the latter has hewed pretty much to its original sense, representing one of the most dreaded certainties known to humankind.

Duty has almost the same double meaning. The adjective *due* is from the past participle of the French verb *devoir,* to owe, and the noun was formed by adding the *-ty,* in the same fashion–in both a linguistic and qualitative sense–as *cruelty* and *penalty.*

Poor old Walpole, who was actually noted for his low-taxation policies, got in hot water over an attempt to scotch smuggling by imposing an excise duty on tobacco and wine. *Excise* in the tax sense is not related to *excise* as in "cut out," as natural as the analogy may seem. The tax version is a corruption of the Latin *ad* and *census* (tax). In the Middle Ages, corruption of words was almost as common as knavery among tax collectors and other public officials. Thank goodness things have changed.

Here's how Dr. Samuel Johnson's famous dictionary defined excise: "A hateful tax levied upon commodities, and adjudged not by the common judges of property, but wretches hired by those to whom excise is paid." William Cobbett, a dedicated and articulate bugbear of governments in the early 19th century, divided the populace into two categories–taxpayers and tax-eaters.

All this won't make budgets any easier to take, but it might help you understand the pain.

Some words can have two exactly opposite meanings. Take "spear-carrier." In one sense he has a minor role and in another he is regarded as a leading player. It's a double-edged sword.

Beware the two-faced contronym

Word watchers are a lot like bird watchers, except that the former have dryer feet and wetter wit. Both are obsessive collectors, always on the lookout for rare species–a preoccupation that accounts for their often distrait countenances.

I count myself among the dry-footed wet-wits, which explains why both my eyebrows and my spirits soared the other day when I saw the headline on a column in a Toronto tabloid (original meaning: a small, easily swallowed pill). The column was about U.S. Republican presidential aspirant Pat Buchanan, and the headline was "Spear carrier on the right." A few weeks before that, a story in another Toronto paper referred to Joe Clark as "the spear-carrier" in the federal government's crusade to find a constitutional holy grail.

Both uses of the metaphor conflicted not only with my understanding of the term, but also with the sense in another story that described a member of the Prime Minister's Office as "only a spear-carrier" in a campaign to discredit an uncomplimentary book about Brian Mulroney.

Beyond doubt, what I had here was a splendid and unusual specimen of a "Janus word," named after the

Roman gatekeeper of heaven, who had two faces so he could keep an eye on everybody, coming or going. Such words are also known as contronyms, because they have directly opposing meanings.

The older, pejorative sense of *spear-carrier,* almost always preceded by "only a" or "a mere," is a theatrical metaphor meaning a minor player, one of the crowd, an underling and, by extension, a nobody. Even in this sense, it's not all that old; the earliest citation in the *Oxford English Dictionary* is 1960.

As applied to Joe Clark and Pat Buchanan, the epithet carried an opposite thrust: the leading player, proponent, or hero. Mine was not the first sighting. The *OED* has a 1967 passage from *The New York Times* saying that Dr. Martin Luther King, Jr., had "emerged as the public spear-carrier of a civil disobedience program." This second and contrary sense probably results from confusion with both *spearhead,* whose figurative sense of leadership dates from the last century, and *standard-bearer,* which was a metaphor for "champion" more than 400 years ago.

Patience and hawklike vision yielded another specimen recently. In her column about magazines, Kate Fillion described the editor of *Esquire* magazine as a "ladies' man" in the sense that, under his 14-month leadership, the erstwhile symbol of male chauvinism had become less sexist and more understanding of and sympathetic to women's issues.

All the lexicons at my disposal define "lady's man" or "ladies' man" as a male who seeks and enjoys the company of women. I'm not sure this definition goes far enough, because in my own understanding of the expression there is an unmistakable connotation of rake, libertine, womanizer, or even gay Lothario, if such a description makes sense any more. On the other hand, maybe I'm mixing this up with "lady-killer," but in either case, it's a far cry from the feminist-sympathizing sense conveyed by Ms. Fillion.

You can understand my excitement over this discovery, because Janus words are as rare as whooping cranes. The reason is that when a word develops conflicting meanings, one of them usually becomes obsolete. Janus words have given us a fine example of peaceful coexistence.

Probably the best known is *cleave,* which can mean either adhering very closely or severing in no uncertain terms. I have always been of two minds about whether the expression *cleft stick* was an ingenious pun. Another standby is *sanction,* by which action you can either endorse something or disapprove of it in a more or less official way.

Some of our simplest and oldest words have split personalities too. The preposition *with* can mean either for or against, depending on whether you're arguing *with* the school debating team or *with* your spouse. *Fast* may mean speedy or absolutely immobile. When five people have *left* the room, how many are *left?* We *dust* roses to put something on them, and furniture to take something off. While steel is *tempered,* or hardened, we often *temper,* or soften, harsh words.

Now that you're finished, would you say you *scanned* this article (examined it thoroughly) or *scanned* it (skipped over hastily)?

Be careful when it comes to Perilous Pairs. Making the wrong choice between words that look alike often can have humorous, ironic, or downright embarrassing results.

One's right, the other's wrong

Finding a spelling error or grammatical lapse in the Imperial Oil *Review* is as rare as a frown on Murray Westgate's physiognomy.

The *Review*, in its 74th year of publication, is one of Canada's oldest magazines. It is also, by far, Canada's best magazine bargain. The price has not increased since the beginning—it's still free.

What's more, it's a high-quality, albeit low-octane, quarterly. Its readers don't look to it for controversy, sharp-tongued opinion, or even hand-wringing viewing-with-alarm. They know, when it arrives, like a smile in a letterbox otherwise bristling with exigencies of every kind, that it will contain a half-dozen engaging, informative, literate, and highly readable stories about the cultural, social, or business life of this country.

So the discovery of a rare solecistic clanger in the pages of the Review is not the occasion for gleeful "gotchas." Rather it is an excuse—using the old exception-proves-the-rule device—to give the publication a plug (management is doing a readership survey). It is also an excuse to write this article, which is about a phenomenon I call Treacherous Twosomes, or Perilous Pairs.

The aberrant error is in the Fall 1991 issue of the *Review.* A story about the eminent medical researcher Dr. Fraser Mustard says: "He made his mark in research on hardening of the arteries and has accumulated a forbidding list of degrees and honours in the years since."

It seems unlikely in the extreme that the writer meant to describe Dr. Mustard's kudos and assorted credentials as *frightening, repulsive, scary, repellant, alarming, disagreeable, menacing, horrifying, hideous, grisly, sinister, threatening,* or *grim.*

But these are all synonyms of *forbidding,* from the Old English *forbeodan* for *prohibit, bar, deny, challenge, exclude, restrain.* What the writer probably meant was *formidable,* a word we cribbed from the French about 500 years ago. Its root is in the Latin *formidare* (to fear or dread), but modern usage has lent it some highly positive connotations such as *redoubtable, monumental, awesome,* and *excellent beyond compare.* We've seen the same sort of ameliorative usage in the adverbs *awfully, terribly,* and *frightfully.*

Terrible Twosomes are words that look tantalizingly alike, but have quite different meanings. The wrong choice may have humorous or ironic results. Common confusions between such look-alikes as *imply/infer, affect/effect, its/it's, farther/further,* and *fewer/less* don't count.

Years ago I attended an awards banquet whose lowlight was an excruciatingly tedious discourse by a guest notable. The person assigned the task of thanking the speaker was, I'm sure, trying to be gracious when he extended enthusiastic gratitude for a "particularly enervating address." He meant *energetic* or *energizing,* of course, even though his choice was both more candid and more accurate.

I've had many chuckles at reading or hearing that someone has "run the entire gambit" of something or other. It invariably conjures up for me the image of a wild-eyed neo-Cossack, frustrated beyond endurance, galloping all over a chessboard, not to mention his opponent.

The required word here is *gamut,* a Latin contraction of the Greek musical notes *gamma* and *ut.* It came to mean the whole range of notes of the diatonic scale, the basis of modern music, and very likely also the catatonic scale, the basis of modern rock. Eventually, *gamut* broadened its dominion to signify the entire soup-to-nuts, A-to-Z, lock-stock-and-barrel, of anything.

Gambit has a history too uncertain and too complicated to go into here. It has a special meaning in chess, often associated with an opening strategy involving some sacrifice to gain a greater advantage. By the mid-19th century it was being used to mean any old ploy or clever tactic in anything from war to a domestic spat.

The wrong half of a Perilous Pair can pop up anywhere. Have you been to a meeting and had to suppress a guffaw when the boss heaped fulsome (exaggerated, disgusting, foul, insincere) praise on a sycophantic underling for an ingenuous (naive) and artful (sly, cunning, deceitful) presentation–especially considering the enormity (monstrous wickedness) of the task and the fact that so many obstacles mitigated (eased, softened) against the project?

Do you get slightly *nauseous* (sic) or snort *contemptibly* when some *imminent* politician is *phased* by the *simplistic* problem of keeping her flotsams *discreet* from her jetsams? Then you are a person of high *principal* and great *perspicuity,* and I *complement* you for it. Just don't *flout* it *noisomely.*

But do tell the folks at Imperial Oil how much you like the *Review,* rare warts and all.

The Inuit have a whole blizzard of words for different types of snow, right? Wrong. Their language doesn't have many more ways of describing solid precipitation than English does.

*

A snow job on the white stuff

There's a delightful Newfoundlandish expression for the last (it's hoped) snowfall of winter. It usually occurs around St. Patrick's Day, give or take two months, and it's called Sheila's brush.

Newfoundlanders, not usually taken to fanciful language, have other descriptive terms for solid precipitation, including *silver thaw, dwy, glidder, batch,* and *shatter.* In this plenitude of snow words, they may rival the vocabulary of the Inuit, who, as everybody knows, have oodles of words for the white stuff.

Or do they? The common belief in a megaplicity of Inuit snow words is challenged in *The Great Eskimo Vocabulary Hoax,* a recent book by California linguist Geoffrey K. Pullum. It seems the myth began in 1911, when U.S. anthropologist Franz Boas "revealed" that Arctic Aboriginal peoples have many words for snow, and that these words grew from distinct roots. The word for "falling snow," he wrote, is different from the one for "snow on the ground," and both are different from "drifting snow" and so on.

Three decades later, an influential amateur linguist in Connecticut picked up the theme. "We have the same word for falling snow, snow on the ground, snow packed hard like ice, slushy snow, wind-driven flying snow—whatever the situation might be," wrote Benjamin Lee Whorf in a technical journal. "To an Eskimo, this all-inclusive word would be unthinkable; he would say that falling snow, slushy snow, and so on, are sensually and operationally different, different things to contend with; he uses different words for them and other kinds of snow."

Leaving aside Mr. Whorf's inaccurate observations on his own language (we *do* have different words for snow, such as sleet, hail, slush, blizzard, flurry, graupel, not to mention Sheila's brush), the suggestion was that Inuit people had many different words for solid precipitation, and that really started the snowball rolling, if you get the drift.

Since then, the number of Inuit snow-words has been put at anywhere from seven to 400. Every first-year linguistics student absorbs the "fact [sic] that the Inuit language has far more words for snow than does English, while Arabic has a far richer vocabulary pertaining to sand," to quote from one Canadian textbook. The misinformed consensus is that, whatever the exact number, it's anywhere from a shovelful to an avalanche.

Laura Martin, an anthropologist at Cleveland State University, explained the myth's appeal in a presentation to the American Anthropological Association in 1982. First, she said, it's logical to us that Inuit people, to whom snow is so significant, should have many words for differentiating its types, textures, colours, and configurations. Second, people in so-called advanced cultures "are prepared to believe anything about such an unfamiliar and peculiar group."

Professor Pullum says the whole affair is "an embarrassing saga of scholarly sloppiness and popular eagerness to embrace exotic facts about other people's languages without seeing the evidence."

I'd still be nodding in earnest agreement if I hadn't encountered, in another of his highly readable essays, this gratuitously outrageous generalization: "In Quebec, the francophone majority want a French First policy, and in the rest of Canada, French . . . is treated with utter contempt." The only evidence he mentions to support this blanket condemnation of anglophone Canada is a bilingual sign he saw in Vancouver, which contained spelling errors in French.

Anyway, as Professor Pullum points out, pinning down the actual number of Inuit words for snow is impossible. What do you count, and where do you stop? Inuit languages and dialects have many more grammatical endings than English, and a more prolific system of "derivational morphology," or ways of forming word offshoots. Moreover, some words become notionally, then lexically, associated with snow. The word for "home-building material" may in some contexts mean "packable snow ideal for making igloos," but it still wouldn't be a snow-word derivative.

Alana Johns, an Inuktitut specialist in the linguistics department at Memorial University in St. John's, says the Inuit vocabulary has a few more differently rooted words for snow than English does. Some examples are the Inuvialuit *aqiluraq* for "light, soft snow," *mauya* for "deep, soft snow," and the enchantingly echoic verb *qiqaaqtuaq,* which translates as "making a squeaking noise when walking on snow."

But Dr. Johns says she can't see what all the fuss is about. "The numbers aren't that significant to a linguist," she says, "but the obsession with them might make a fascinating folklore thesis."

Note: I would like to express my indebtedness to Harold Paddock, also of the linguistics department at Memorial University, who supplied those wonderful Newfoundland words for snow.

This famous name is synonymous with dictionaries, but it's not a trademark. Any publishing house can slap the esteemed moniker on its latest edition. And many do.

*

The tangled web of Webster

What's in a name? If the name is Webster and it's on a dictionary, the answer is: not a whole lot.

Almost a century after the surname of one of history's greatest lexicographers passed into the public domain, the name Webster still defines "dictionary," at least in North America. What's more, in most people's minds it also denotes high quality and, though this is often far from the truth, it accounts for the name's popularity among publishers who have less family connection to Noah Webster than to the Noah of early zoological fame.

For those who still haven't got the word–and an unscientific survey of my friends, family, and colleagues indicates this is a lot of people–Webster is not a trademark. If you published a book of word definitions tomorrow and called it the "Webster's *Globe and Mail* Reader's Dictionary," you might be in some trouble with the *Globe,* but you'd be on safe ground with the Webster's part.

The dictionary business has always been bedeviled by copyright squabbles, mainly because of the universal nature of the subject. Many early lexicographers borrowed freely from their predecessors' work, and added some new material to make their product look unique, prompting one historian to characterize the industry's development as "incremental plagiarism."

The latest legal hassle ended when a U.S. District Court jury in New York ordered Random House to pay nearly $2.3 million to Merriam-Webster Inc. (the "real" Webster company) for trademark infringement.

Merriam-Webster sued after Random House, which had proudly resisted the marketing appeal of the Webster name for decades, succumbed to the temptation and published its *Random House Webster's New College Dictionary.* Its dimensions, its red dust jacket, and the word "Webster's" in big white letters on the spine made it look suspiciously like the Merriam-Webster company's *Webster's Ninth New Collegiate Dictionary,* latest edition of the best-selling book the firm first published in 1898.

The jury didn't mince words. It found that the external design of the Random House book was an intentional attempt to confuse buyers, and represented a "wanton disregard of the rights of Merriam-Webster."

The case didn't hinge on the word *Webster.* That battle was lost years earlier. But Merriam-Webster does hold a trademark right to the word *Collegiate,* when it's applied to a dictionary. The jury felt Random House's use of the word *College,* along with other distinctive "trade dress" found traditionally on its rival's books, constituted unfair competition.

Merriam-Webster (owned since 1964 by Encyclopaedia Britannica, just to complicate things further) is the undisputed corporate heir to Noah Webster, the multitalented, multilingual lexicographer who published his landmark *American Dictionary of the English Language* in 1828, a full century before the great *Oxford English Dictionary* was completed. Interestingly, Noah himself declined to put his name on his own dictionary.

After Webster died in 1843, the printing brothers George and Charles Merriam acquired the rights to his dictionary. The Merriam boys knew more about word books than law books, apparently, because by the turn of the century bookstore shelves were displaying several pseudo-Websters, and the company's legal attempts to stop the spread failed. A U.S. court ruling in the 1940s removed all doubt that Webster had become a household word.

After all these years the name *Webster* still has marketing magic. It appears on dozens of dictionaries whose quality ranges from very good to farcical. At the low end, there's a "Student's Webster Dictionary" that is a whopping 48 pages short, and a "New Concise Webster's Dictionary" that has only two entries under "X" (*x-ray* n., and *x-ray* v.). Published in August was a wallet-sized "New Webster's Pocket Pal Dictionary" whose boast of containing "more than 90,000 words and meanings" is substantiated only by counting every word in the book, including those in the definitions.

Oxford University Press, with a later start in these matters, has had more success in protecting its name. Nobody else publishes an *Oxford* dictionary. On the other hand, and in a slightly different genre, the words *Roget's Thesaurus* are, like *Webster,* public property.

Perhaps the most curious thing of all in this titular tangle is this: While everyone involved agrees *Webster* is generic, you won't find it defined that way in your "Webster's"–or in any other dictionary. The *Penguin Canadian Dictionary* comes closest, defining it as "an American English dictionary." The rest give it as an obsolete word for "weaver."

It's too bad that a private member's bill promoting understandable English in laws and regulations hasn't got a hope of being passed. It's also too bad about the way the bill is written.

Sharpening the statutory instruments

The Honourable (not to mention Estimable) Ian Waddell, NDP Member of Parliament for Port Moody-Coquitlam and Plain Speaking, is at it again. For the second time in two years he is trying to get legislation aimed at making federal laws and regulations understandable to ordinary Canadians.

Now, before we make the welkin ring with huzzahs, hear-hears, and maybe even a hallelujah, keep in mind that this private member's bill—sponsored as it is by a member of Her Majesty's Loyal Third Party—has approximately zilch chance of becoming a law of the land.

Mind you, the bill's prognosis, unpropitious though it may be, is not improved by the fact that it suffers from the very disease it is intended to treat. This is not Mr. Waddell's fault, however. The bill was drafted by the House of Commons Legal Service, and tradition dies hard.

The giveaway is in the title: "*An Act to promote the use of plain language in federal statutes, statutory instruments and regulations.*" My guess is that the average Canadian—or even the above average one—doesn't know a "statutory instrument" from a mandatory mouth-organ, but would recognize a spade anywhere if it were so-called. And why the timorous "promote"? A brass-tacks reformer would have used a title something like: "An Act requiring plain, unadulterated, nonlegal language in any written piece of federal falderal that may affect Canadians in any way."

Section 3. of the draft begins: "*There is hereby established a Committee called the Language Review Committee consisting of three members from each political party in the House of Commons . . .* " Why backward runs this sentence? Aren't the words *a Committee called* superfluous? Are there nonpolitical parties in the House? And do we really need the archaism *hereby?* A useful pamphlet published by the State Bar Association of California, called *Are You Misunderstood? Try Plain English,* says: "Omit obsolete formalisms and old English phrases. These include such words as . . . *hereby.*"

It gets worse. Section 5. says: "*No payments shall be made out of the Consolidated Revenue Fund to defray expenses necessary for the implementation of this Act without the authority of an appropriation made by Parliament for such purposes.*" Plain language translation: "Not a dad-burned red cent of taxpayers' money will be spent to put this act into effect without Parliament's say-so."

Section 7. of the draft: "*The Language Review Committee may engage on a temporary basis, the services of persons having a specialized knowledge of any matter relating to the work of the Committee to advise and assist the Committee in the performance of its duties.*" Suggested plain language: "The Committee will need help. So it may occasionally enlist the services of expert consultants, such as word columnists from national journals (stipend not to exceed $500 an hour)."

Seriously, Mr. Waddell deserves all the support he can get for this movement. It is a principle of our system that ignorance of the law is no excuse for breaking one.

"So if people are to be responsible," says the MP, "they should be able to understand the law. Besides, this is a very democratic process. It forces legislators to say what they mean." (Some Hon. Mems.: "Oh, oh.")

Section 6. says the committee will review bills and then "*shall recommend and report to the House of Commons any changes, which in its opinion, will simplify the language* . . . " Is it necessary to both recommend *and* report? And on whose opinion other than its own would the committee base recommendations for change?

The real zinger is section 10. (a), which says: "*This Act does not apply to a Government Bill where the government House Leader advises the House of Commons after the introduction of the Bill in the House, that the Bill is exempt from review by the Language Review Committee.*"

If I read that correctly–and, being an average Canadian, this is no easy task–legislation proposed by the government does not have to be referred to the plain language watchdog committee if the government House Leader decides to exempt it from such scrutiny. Since bills introduced by the government are the ones that usually get enacted, this means that most laws will still be impenetrable.

"If the law says that," to quote Dickens's Mr. Bumble, "the law is a ass, a idiot."

An "apron" used to be a "napron" until the "n" started to migrate. The word is a victim of Consonantal Drift Syndrome, something that has afflicted many other nouns over the years.

N-shift: a nugly phenomenon

When a *Globe and Mail* headline writer capped a winter fun story with "An ice time was had by all," was it just a playful urge to pun? Or was there something deeper, more primal, more sinister at work? Was it, in short, a new occurrence of the rare, insidious, and little known Consonantal Drift Syndrome?

An instance of this heretofore unnamed phenomenon, which I informally call "N-Shift," has not been observed by morphologists for centuries. But it is well known to them, and feared, for when an innocent word is caught in the Consonantal Drift, they know it will never again be the same.

The harmless, homely *apron* was a victim. It used to begin with an "n" as this line from *The Tale of Beryn* (ca.1400) attests: "With hir napron fair, she wypid sofft hir eyen." That spelling (of apron, at least) was logical because the word came to us from the Old French *naperon,* a diminutive of *nappe* or table-napkin. Through carelessness, "a napron" eventually became "an apron." Relics of the old form survive in our *napkin, napery,* and the surname *Napier.*

The lowly *adder* and the humble but useful *auger*

were similarly decapitated. In 1366, Sir John Mandeville, the first English travel writer, described some creeping dangers this way: "Thei maken a maner of hissynge, as a neddre dothe." The Old English *naedre,* for serpent, went through several spellings before arriving at *nadder* in the 15th century. Sloppy pronunciation with the indefinite article turned "a nadder" into "an adder."

The American expression "mad as a cut snake" may have had a forerunner in "mad as an adder." This in turn gave us "mad as a hatter" because of the similarity of sound, and because hat-makers often suffered dementia through their use of chemicals.

An *auger,* formerly a *nauger,* was originally a *nafugar* (wheel-nave piercer) in Anglo-Saxon. It blew its top some time in the 15th century. The usually unflappable *umpire* began to lose his head around 1400. Until then the word was *noumpere,* from the Middle French *nonper,* or "not equal." Again, incorrect division between the article and the noun resulted in the modern word.

A 15th century English cookery-book contained this recipe instruction: "Take ye numbles of Venysoun, an cutte hem smal whyle they ben raw." *Numbles* were the entrails of deer. While the upper classes dined on venison, the servants were given the *numbles,* which they usually baked into a pie. By transposition, *numble-pie* became *umble-pie.* Influenced by both the association with society's lower orders and the historical English confusion with the letter "h", *humble-pie* evolved, and to eat it meant to be abjectly apologetic and humiliated.

Orange had already been pared by the time it arrived in English. In Arabic it was *naranj,* in Persian *narang,* and in Hindi *narangi*–all similar to the modern Spanish *naranja.* The "N-Shift" occurred in both Italian (originally *una narancia,* now just *arancia*) and French (earlier *une narange*). It's speculated that the fruit's golden colour may have accounted for the eventual "*or*-ange" spelling in both French and English.

In several cases the "n" travelled the other way. A *nickname* was once an *eke-name,* an augmented or increased name. A *notch* at one time was an *otch,* from the Old French *oche,* meaning "notch."

If you're a crossword puzzle fan, you know that *eft* is another word for *newt,* right? Wrong. They're the same word. *Ewt* was another spelling of *eft,* a small member of the amphibian order *Salamandridae,* and became *newt* some time around the 16th century. During the same period, folk etymology was toying with changing *idiot* into *nidiot,* further corrupted to *nidget,* but the old spelling fought back and survived. *Uncle* and *aunt* were imperilled too, appearing in Shakespeare as *nuncle* and *naunt* (in these cases, the "n" slipped over from the possessive pronoun "mine"), but they too prevailed.

Sometimes words just got squished together. *Alone* came from the earlier phrase "all one," and *another* was originally "an other," and occasionally, yes, "a nother." The verb to *don* was to "do on," and *doff* was–guess what?–the opposite.

Now, if you'll excuse me, I've got an agging headache. And the spell-checker on my word processor is in a nugly mood.

PART FOUR

*

Shifting sands of meaning

Many of the words we commonly use had quite different meanings to our linguistic ancestors—some of them a lot more polite than their current connotations. There are also many delightful archaisms that are definitely worth dusting off for new duty.

We seldom hear such stout epithets as "scoundrel," "blackguard," or "knave" any more. It's a pity because they're insults with long and (sort of) honourable histories.

*

A varlet nowadays is hard to find

Twice within a recent week the word *scoundrel* appeared in local newspaper headlines–once to describe an arrested Soviet KGB chief and the other in reference to a break-in at the home of a former baseball manager. However appropriate in these disparate contexts, the apparent renaissance of a potent old English word engulfed this unregenerate archaist with waves of nostalgia.

Scoundrel is one of a fusty family of stout English epithets that, while not quite as one with the dodo, are rarely seen in modern writing. For me they spell instant romance, conjuring up pre-Kevin Costner scenes of chivalrous conflict in which the air is rent by the clash of steel and shouts of "knave" and "varlet" and "blackguard." Somehow, "scum-bag" and "sleaze-ball" just don't have the same effect.

No one is sure of *scoundrel*'s origin, although a popular theory relates it to the French *escondre,* to "abscond." Despite its obsolescence, most people would know that it means a low and despicable sort of chap whose scruples could be computed on the fingers of one hand, with some to spare. In other words, a rascal and a bounder.

Rascal is also of uncertain origin but may have descended from the Old French *rascaille,* for scrapings, dregs, or rabble. *Rascallion,* also rendered *rapscallion* and *rascabillion,* is, according to Oxford, "rascal with a fanciful ending." They all denote a mean wretch or *scalawag*–another word whose ancestors are, perhaps all to the good, lost in history.

Some of these insults didn't start that way. *Rogue* (not, despite its appearance, of French derivation) was in the mid-16th century a mildly derisory term for an idle vagrant, but soon came to be synonymous with a dishonest, unprincipled person, or worse. Similarly a *blackguard* was originally one of the lowest menials in a royal household, responsible for cleaning soot-covered pots and pans. Usage broadened its scope to include all kinds of criminals and miscreants.

Blackguard's evolution attests to the existence of class discrimination in Merrie Olde England, as does that of *varlet,* a variation of valet. Originally an attendant or knight's page, *varlet* soon developed the same scornful connotation as *villain.* A *villain* (from Latin *villa,* or farm) was at first no more than a low-born country lout. Seven centuries debased it to the point that one could hardly call anyone worse.

Knave and *cad* betray intolerance of another kind–a prejudice against male youth. *Knave,* which may or may not be related to the German *knabe,* or boy, began its English career as nothing more sinister than a male child. Before long it was applied to youthful servants and then to male menials of all ages. At that point it entered the class-hate stream and eventually took on all the baggage of deceit and disrepute.

Cad comes from *cadet* (from Latin, "little head"), which about 350 years ago meant only a younger son or brother. At about the same time that *cadet* took on the meaning of unpaid officer trainee, its abbreviation *cad* came to mean a lower grade assistant to a tradesman such as a bricklayer. Another developing sense was that of a boy who waited about for chance employment, or an odd-job man. From this sense evolved *caddie.*

It's a short leap from *cad* to *bounder* (someone beyond the bounds of decent behaviour), but this is too new a word (late 19th century) to evoke the same romance as *knave* and *varlet.*

The list of more classical put-downs is by no means exhausted. We haven't even touched on *cutpurse* (a common thief, originally one who cut the straps of a victim's purse and ran off with it), *scapegrace* (someone who has somehow managed to completely escape the grace of God), *vaurien* (a good-for-nothing, from the French for "worth nothing") and *ne'er-do-well* (which is self-explanatory).

And–Gad! sir–my space runneth out before I can even mention *mountebank* or *charlatan* or . . .

Once upon a time a hussy was a housewife, egregious meant distinguished, and a rustler was the same as a hustler. Then they all suffered the dreaded fate of pejoration.

When meaning goes downmarket

Suppose you're leaving a party. You thank the host for an egregious time, and tell him that his wife–"the hussy"–simply filled you with lust. You call him a sly rustler and congratulate him on having such a specious harlot for a daughter. "I may be just a lewd snob," you say finally, "but this party had a real stench to it that I resent, and I really hope I can retaliate."

Question: Do you think you would be invited back? Not likely in this day and age, but at one or another time during the evolution of our language, all of those insulting terms were either highly complimentary or at least neutral.

Egregious, which now means "about as bad as it gets," once meant exactly the opposite–remarkably good, distinguished. It's from Latin for "out of" and "flock," and meant standing out from or towering above the rest. It went from a strong positive to a definite negative through a usage phenomenon the experts call pejoration or degradation, and I call "going to rat-spit."

I was reminded of this process of word evolution when the Social Studies department of *The Globe and Mail*'s Facts and Arguments page recently noted that the word *cheater* once signified nothing more than a rent collector. In this case, it's easy to see how the downgrading came about; with others it's not so simple.

The experts guess that *egregious* hit the skids when some people began using it ironically or sarcastically–in the same way you might say "that's just great" when you mean it's the pits.

Hussy started out merely as a familiar form of housewife or thrifty woman. Over the years it gradually worsened to mean a woman of improper, pert, or mischievous behaviour, or a minx. *Housewife* may in fact be going through a process of pejoration today.

Lust, a fine Old English word, at first denoted pleasure or delight. From there it moved on to desire, appetite, or relish and finally gave way to the modern meaning of sexual or libidinous desire, or animal passion. You can still use the adjective *lusty* in a non-insulting way if you mean singing or prose that is healthy or vigorous. But the noun *lust* is bad, even if it's only in your heart, as Jimmy Carter will attest.

A *rustler* wasn't always a horse thief. In the 19th century United States, it also was a complimentary word for *hustler*–an energetic, bustling person. *Sly* once meant skilful or knowledgeable, as well as cleverly deceitful. These two prove the prime rule of pejoration: If a word has a nice meaning and a nasty meaning, the nasty one will almost always prevail.

Specious originally meant beautiful and pleasing to the eye. Of flowers and birds it meant showy or gaudy, and eventually this sense deteriorated to signify something outwardly fair, attractive, or plausible, but in reality lacking those qualities, or fallacious.

A *harlot* for a daughter? Why not? This crib from Old French has had many meanings, from vagabond and beggar to a young person of either sex. But for a period in the 15th century, it also meant a ballet dancer or actress. Since women in the performing arts were not high on the social register, the word took a big dip in the pop charts and ended up meaning strumpet.

At one point there was no taint attached to *lewd.* It merely meant you were a layman, not in holy orders. It naturally developed into unlettered and ignorant, then common, base, or ill-bred. From there it took on a meaning of naughty (which itself once meant only "possessing nothing" or poor), and then it was full speed astern to its present sense of lascivious, unchaste, and "dirty."

A *snob* was once a cobbler. The nobs at Cambridge made it a slang word for townsman, or "not one of us." For a period well into the 19th century, it meant just an ordinary person with no pretensions to rank.

Early on, *stench* stood for odour or aroma, often a sweet one. In the 17th century, to *resent* something was to appreciate it. And until about 200 years ago, to *retaliate* was to return a favour, not to get even.

I hope there's nothing libellous here, because, after all, *libel* is from the diminutive of the Latin *liber* (book) and used to mean a little book, or a short treatise.

A "distaff" was a cleft stick that held unspun flax or wool. Since women did the spinning, it came to mean women in general. Would I spin you a yarn?

*

Intricate threads of meaning

Even if you're not into pay-as-you-play equestrianism, you may have noticed that a Canadian female thoroughbred named Dance Smartly won the 1991 "Distaff" event at the prestigious Breeders' Cup at Louisville, Kentucky.

It wasn't the horse's accomplishment that struck me, but the curious use of the word *distaff.*

Distaff is one of those words most of us take in by osmosis. We know it has something to do with women or wives, but we couldn't explain why, even if our marriages depended on it. I don't know about you, but when this happens to me, I emulate Dance Smartly and gallop to the nearest reliable dictionary.

The *dis* part is not a negative prefix but an Old English word meaning a bunch of flax. A *distaff* was originally a rod with a cleft end for holding unspun flax or wool. From this, threads were tweaked and twisted to be fed into a spinning wheel.

The person who did the tweaking and twisting almost invariably was–you guessed it–the medieval missus. Back then, Eaton's and The Bay had not yet been invented. So women did a lot of spinning, followed by a lot of weaving and knitting–that is, when they weren't cooking or washing. So the distaff became a symbol of women's work, then evolved into a representation of women in general.

Usages along these lines are found in writings as old as Chaucer and Shakespeare, and as recently as Thomas Carlyle in the last century. It should not surprise anyone that some of the uses betray a traditional male pretension to superiority. This line from English essayist and society poet Winthrop Mackworth Praed (1802–39) illustrates the point:

> His delicate hand
> Seemed fitter for the distaff than the spear.

Praed managed to work in one of the non-distaff terms. For many years, *spear* or *sword* was the male counterpart of the symbolic distaff. Why women got the short end of the stick and men were symbolized by heroic utensils of war instead of, say, a plough or a masonry hod, is not hard to guess at. In any case, the weapons' symbolism for men fell into disuse except in a couple of modern macho senses, mostly unmentionable.

But *distaff* did stick, and by the 1600s even a Saint Distaff had been invented and given a special day. St. Distaff's Day (you could look it up) was January 7, the day after the Feast of the Epiphany, when women were supposed to end their holiday revelries and get back to the spinning wheels. This, too, is recorded in English literature, in a poem by Robert Herrick in 1648 titled "St. Distaff's Day." It contains this line:

> Give Saint Distaff all the right,
> Then bid Christmas sport good night.

Spinning was such a pervasive activity in the late Middle Ages, and so exclusively associated with women, that it produced another word on the distaff side: *spinster*.

It first meant any women who did spinning, but particularly those who did it for a living. Typically the latter were registered for payroll and other official purposes as, for example, Jane Doe, Spinster. Since career women were usually single women, *spinster* came to mean an unmarried female, and by the 18th century the term had legal status.

Inevitably some louts used the term disparagingly—especially if the woman in question was getting a bit beyond conventional marrying age. By the time *spinster* worked its way up into the 20th century, it also carried the connotation of plain, older, and not only unmarried but unmarriageable. In this era of covert marital status, *spinster* is heading for the scrap heap, along with such other quaint obsolescences as *maiden aunt*.

Things are not so simple with *bachelor.* Experts disagree on this word's roots but the majority view is that it descends from the Latin *vacca* for—of all things—cow. By the Late Latin period this had become *bacca* and had spawned *baccalia* for herd of cows, and *baccalarius* for the young farmhand who tended them. From there came the French *bachelier* and the 16th century English *bachelour,* which later dropped the "u."

The word progressed to mean a young knight of the lowest order, a junior member of a trade guild, someone who holds the lowest university degree, and an unmarried man.

Bachelor does not seem to have developed the same stigma as *spinster.* But that—to get back to the theme—is a horse of a different yarn.

Some of the feedback I get is nasty, brutish, and short. Other reactions, however, are more thoughtful and considerably more interesting. A sampling . . .

*

Pejorated, jingled, and bedizened

The second "c" in *anticlimactically* went AWOL in a piece I wrote recently, and although it may be too late to stanch the torrent of frenzied fulminations from readers slavering to notch a "gotcha," let me assure ye of little faith that the error did not emanate from this humble wordmonger. It was–if I may use that last refuge of the journalistic scoundrel–a typo.

Actually, very little of the feedback to my column is of the slavering variety, and then it's usually nasty and brutish, but short.

Not so the epistles of Joe Keogh, an English teacher at Niagara University and one-time researcher for Marshall McLuhan. Mr. Keogh, who averages three single-spaced pages and approximately 17.6 thought-provoking ideas per letter, said my recent mention of *jingled* as a euphemism for tipsy shed new light on his studies of Edgar Allan Poe. Poe, notes Mr. Keogh, was "famous for his jingling rhymes and his addiction to mimicking the sounds of all sorts of bells, whether wedding, fire, or funeral," and was "no less famous for his addiction to spirituous liquors."

Another teacher, David Ingham of the University of Lethbridge, wrote: "I taught for the first time this fall a first-year (freshperson?) course called 'The World of

Words,' and was most happy to have at hand a weekly column which was invariably appropriate as class material, even for the most 'Englishly challenged' of my students–and invariably a delight for their instructor."

Professor Ingham also sent along some of his favourite oxymorons, one of which I'm still trying to figure out: "Toronto Life."

Some of the response is by word of mouth, in more ways than one. My dentist claims he doesn't recognize a lot of the words I use, and that makes us even. Not that I get much of a chance to use any when we meet on his turf. Like all practitioners of his ilk, he waits until he has my mouth comfortably jammed with suction tube, cylindrical cotton pads, mirror, drill, and nine-tenths of his fingers before engaging me in conversation.

"You used the word *pejoration,*" he italicized recently. "Is there such a word? Is there a verb *to pejorate?* Am I *hurting* you? Could you speak *more clearly?*"

Here is a translation of the answers I murgled to him: "Yes. Yes. Yes. No."

Pejorate means to worsen, the opposite of *ameliorate,* to improve. *Pejoration* is the noun, and once it's happened to you you're in the *pejority.* Now here's the big bonus, one of those serendipitous rewards for dallying with a dictionary: *Pejorist* is also a word. It's not someone who worsens, but someone who espouses *pejorism,* the belief that the world is going to hell in a handcart. Throw that into your next cocktail party dialogue.

Jack Meadows wrote from White Rock, B.C., about a column that described the degeneration of the word *hussy,* which was once a simple, harmless diminutive of housewife.

"Do you know," he asked, having the decency not to stuff both hands and sundry utensils into my mouth first, "that as part of their kit, British troops used to be issued with a small cloth roll containing needle, spare buttons, thread, and darning wool, and officially called a *hussif?*"

No, I didn't. *Oxford* (big one, second edition) gives as an obsolete definition of *hussy,* "a case for needles, thread, etc." It also has a separate entry for *hussif,* but dismisses it tersely as a dialectical form of housewife. Next time you see one of these little hussies-away-from-home in a hotel room, you'll know what to call her, er, it.

Here's a peculiar sequel to some recent ruminations on the origin of the feminine adjective *distaff.* You may recall this odd word comes from the Old English *dis,* for flax, and means the rod on a spinning wheel on which a bunch of flax is placed. Within a week of that column, and totally outside the context of it, a friend asked about the meaning of *bedizen.* As it turns out, the "*diz*" part is from that same old word for flax. The verb *dizen* originally meant to place the flax on the distaff, but both *dizen* and *bedizen* later took on the metaphorical sense "to dress up" or "deck out" in vulgar or gaudy fashion.

Dis is really getting to be quite a yarn.

There are some wonderful old words lying around unused—venerable verbs and nouns often a lot more descriptive than their modern counterparts. And there's a flurch of them.

Of sloom, slivens, and scupperloit

The elegantly agnominated John Bentley Mays, visual arts critic, waxed both arch and archaic the other day when he described Toronto's Gardiner Expressway as "that vast raised ribbon of concrete flowing betwixt the downtown towers and Lake Ontario."

Betwixt, an old-fashioned synonym for *between,* is characterized by the *Oxford English Dictionary* as "now somewhat archaic in literary English and chiefly poetical." It has no later citation than 1884, and that is to illustrate the colloquial redundancy *betwixt and between,* which means fair to middling, or so-so.

This, methought, bodes well. If Squire Mays can *creem* (slip something slyly) a grizzled archaism into his *scripitations,* there may be new hope for thousands of other words that have been mouldering in lexicographic limbo.

Pressed among the 22,000 pages of the *OED* second edition are hosts of forgotten but unfaded flowers of seasons past. There are hundreds more in two other charming verbal archives: Charles Mackay's *Lost Beauties of the English Language* (1874), and John Ray's *A Collection of English Words Not Generally Used* (1674).

Using these dormant resources, you could tell your colleagues on Monday that, in spite of a good *sloom* (sound sleep), you awoke at *sparrow-fart* (the breaking of day) feeling totally *forswunk* (worn out). Your cronies *snirtle* (snigger), but you *flurn* (think little of) that, being more concerned about your own *wofare* (opposite of welfare).

Finally they *hurkle* (shrug) and leave. You *strome* (pace back and forth in anger or perplexity), trying to figure out why you feel so *dretched* (tormented) with *mubblefubbles* (low spirits).

It's true you got your feet wet when you weren't *swipper* (nimble) enough to avoid stepping in that big *soss* (mucky puddle). But you can't *threap* (blame) that, because they dried toastily in front of the *bellibleiz* or *lilly-low* (comfortable fire), which you stirred occasionally with the *fruggan* (poker).

Was it something you took for *fuzzen* or *bellytimber* (nourishment)? It was well after *dimps, cockshut,* or *mirkshade* (twilight) when you got home, and rather than *kiss the hare's foot* (be late for dinner and have only the undesirable leftovers), you whipped up some *maw-wallop* (ill-cooked mess of victuals) called *braughwham* (dish of cheese, eggs, oatmeal, and butter boiled together), of which you are so *bloten* (fond). Or maybe you had one *gotch* (large earthen or stone drinking jug) too many of the *clamberscull* (heady liquor). But *barrel fever* (a hangover) is the least of your symptoms.

When you *clomb* out of bed today, you *oke* (past tense of ache) all over and *swat* (ditto of sweat) and *diddered* (shivered) alternately as you *hirpled* (limped; one of only two words that rhyme with purple) to the washroom. You felt *tewly* (sick) in your *slote* (pit of your stomach) and really quite *carked* (anxious, fretful). Your *thropple* (throat) was *roacky* and *roopit* (take a guess; why should I have all the fun?) and you were *growzing* (pre-ague shivering) and altogether *grouty, treaf, frampard, branglesome, fratchy, hickery, toitish, tethy,* and *trunch* (cross and peevish).

There could be no doubt; you had a bad *snurle* (head cold). Today of all days, when you have a *flurch* (multitude) of important things to do and no *scupperloit* (leisure time) to *goyster* (frolic). On top of all this, you forgot to bring a *snotter-clout* (hankie).

This pseudo-anecdote could go on and on. In fact, it just did. The point is that there are lots of useful words lying fallow in our language—not only useful, but in many cases more powerful or more descriptive than the ones we use. Doesn't *argh* (pronounced "arf") make the point better than its modern counterparts, timid and pusillanimous? Aren't *fairy sparks* and *shelfire* more evocative than static electricity? And how about those sponging relatives who know just how to time their visit so that they'll get a free meal? The word for them used to be *smell-feasts.*

Wouldn't you feel better calling idlers and louts *slivens, clinchpoops,* and *callymoochers?* That would make them take notice as they sat there *spoffling* (making busy over something of no consequence). Wouldn't you love to tell a long-winded *lorefather* (pedagogue) to cut the *circumbilivagination?*

So I'm with Squire Mays. Let's forge ahead to the past! If you don't agree, you've got *fluttermice* in your belfry.

"Culprit," whether of the four- or two-legged variety, started out as two words. "The hoi polloi," on the other hand, should indeed be three words, contrary to some peoples' views.

*

Of mice, men . . . and darts from the latter

There might seem at first blush—or even after assiduous analysis—little similarity between a 17th century English member of Parliament and a 20th century mouse that made news a while ago in Smiths Falls, Ontario.

The connection is that they were both called *culprits* in public print. And if you think that's a pretty tenuous foundation on which to build an article, you can move on to the next one.

It was, in fact, in a letter-to-the-editor that *culprit* made one of its rare, early appearances. The year was 1769, and the correspondent to the London *Public Advertiser* was none other than Junius, that incorrigible epistolarian whose hallowed words appear as part of the *Globe*'s editorial page masthead. Junius was discussing Parliament's expulsion of an MP named Wollaston, and his prompt re-election by defiantly loyal constituents. From this, quoth Junius, it seemed that "although he was expelled, he had not rendered himself a culprit too ignominious to sit in parliament." The Smiths Falls mouse got its *culprit* label in a Canadian Press story that told how the varmint gnawed some electrical wires, causing a fire that burned down a mobile home.

Culprit meant the same thing to Junius two and a half centuries ago as it did to the reporter who wrote of the rascally rodent. But the word didn't start out laden with established guilt.

When an accused person in a late medieval courtroom pleaded not guilty, the Clerk of the Crown replied: "*Culpable: prest d'averrer nostre bille.*" Roughly translated, this Anglo-Norman riposte meant, "We think he's guilty (culpable), M'Lud, and we're ready (*prest*) to prove it." Variant spellings of *prest* (equivalent to modern French *prêt*) were *prist* and *prit,* and the clerk's reply was usually abbreviated on the court rolls as "*cul. prit.*"

This gave rise to what the *Oxford English Dictionary* calls "the fortuitous or ignorant running together of two words" to create the new word *culprit.* For a while, this accidental combination was used to describe an as-yet unconvicted accused. But the association with the Latin root *culpa,* for fault or offence, proved too powerful, and by the time Junius tossed off his letter to the *Advertiser,* the principle of innocent-until-proven-guilty had given way to a condemnatory usage.

Speaking of *culpa,* it's *mea.* In "Beware the two-faced contronym" (words that have the same spelling and opposite meanings), *temper* was given as an example–to "soften" as in words or demands, and to "harden" as with steel.

Not so, say metallurgists Don Mills of Toronto and Reginald Tate of Richmond, B.C. Both pointed out that, technically, the tempering process actually softens steel to make it less brittle. This has the effect of "toughening" it, however, which sustains its claim as a contronym for "softening" or "moderating."

And here's a case of *mea culpa, not!* Five other readers brandished their tempered steel swords in my direction for using the phrase *the hoi polloi.* "Since *hoi* already means 'the' this is obviously incorrect," said Paul A. Fulford. And reader Thomas O'Flaherty of London,

Ontario, pleaded: "Say it isn't so! Tell me it's a *lapsus calami* [slip of the pen]! Insist it's a typo!"

Sorry, fellas. No typo. No lapse. No error. The Greek *hoi polloi,* meaning "the many" or "the masses" is an expression that has gained something in the translation. Admittedly, it would be ludicrous to say "the the masses," but that's not what we say. We say "the hoi polloi," and we usually say it with a tinge of scorn. What's more, we've been saying it for 400 years. The *Oxford English Dictionary,* which notes that, "in English [*hoi polloi* is] normally preceded by the definite article even though *hoi* means 'the,'" has citations from Dryden (1668), Byron (1821), James Fenimore Cooper (1837), Frank Lloyd Wright (1932), and others. Gilbert and Sullivan's *Iolanthe* contains this couplet: "*'twill fill with joy and madness stark/the Hoi Polloi (a Greek remark).*"

Brewer's *Dictionary of Phrase and Fable,* first published in 1870, heads its entry "**Hoi Polloi (The).**" For a more up-to-date opinion, Longman's *Guide to English Usage* (1988) says flatly: "It is correct idiomatic English to speak of *the hoi polloi.*"

The common error with *the hoi polloi* is to mistakenly use it for the upper crust, possibly through confusion with *hoity-toity.* The latter has nothing to do with nobility, but one of its senses–assuming, haughty, petulant, huffy–comes close, at least in the view of the hoi polloi.

Today, the word means "well-endowed."
But there was a time when buxom meant obedient,
and women vowed at their weddings
to be buxom to their husbands.

The altared state of being buxom

In a recent Arts Section column, Kate Fillion dissected the controversy surrounding the *Sunday Times*'s sensational serialization of the dirt on Princess Di. Circulation of the usually proper publication shot up by nearly a quarter of a million, and the panting purchasers, according to Ms. Fillion, were "people who would not dream of buying the pint-sized papers that run colour photos of buxom women in the buff."

Never mind the royal bumf; let's look at those odd words, *buxom* and *buff*. It's not often that we get two prize specimens in one sentence.

Buxom has a peculiar past. A while ago—well, about half-a-millennium, actually—when an English bride muttered her vows, she promised, among other things, to be *buxom* to her husband. In doing so, she was not solemnly undertaking to remain "pleasingly plump," or to pump iron in order to maintain her "full figure." She was merely pledging, as brides did until recently, to be obedient.

In the Indo-European language family, *bheug* meant to bend or arch. This spawned a slew of modern English words with the sense of bending, bowing, curving, or forming a ring. They include the verb *bow,* to bend from the waist, and the noun *bow,* as in rainbow, elbow, cupid's bow, and probably akimbo (with arms bent; "arms akimbo" is redundant). The ring or circle sense accounts for bagel, from the German-cum-Yiddish for bracelet; and possibly bee, as in quilting or spelling, but not bumble.

A thing that's bendable or pliable can also be malleable or soft, like a *bog,* which came from the same *bheug* root, via Gaelic. And a person who was pliable might also be compliant, dutiful, or obedient.

In Old English, *bugan* meant to bow, stoop, submit, give way. Obvious cognates in modern German are *biegen,* to bend, and the adjective *biegsam,* flexible. The Old English *bugan* sired the Middle English adjective *buhsum* (rhymes with, but is not related to, bosom–at least, not yet), for obedient.

The subservient sense bowed to broader meanings, including gracious, obliging, amiable, indulgent, and even polite. People who displayed these qualities were usually flexible, good-natured, and easy-going, and by the 17th century the word–by then spelled *buxom* or *buxsome,* and sometimes *bowsum*–was a synonym for blithe or jolly. Milton's *L'Allegro* in 1632 describes a scene of sylvan love-making that results in "a daughter fair, so buxom, blithe and debonair."

At about the same time, the meaning began to shift from temperament or disposition to physical appearance. Since jolliness was often associated with plumpness, the adjective came to mean cheerily chubby, and by the 19th century was being used almost exclusively in connection with women. Sir Walter Scott, in *Peveril of the Peak* (1822), wrote of "a buxom dame about thirty." Both *buxom* and *dame* were politically okay then.

The physical aspect prevailed, and buxom now is used only in the context of women who are "well-endowed," or to use two similar words beginning with the same letters, "busty" or "built." Such a woman need not, by today's definition–and certainly by today's social convention–be obedient, let alone good-natured, easy-going, and jolly. So caution is advised.

Did I almost forget about *buff? Buff* is short for buffalo and "buff-leather" was much used in military coats as far back as the 16th century. In Shakespeare's *Comedy of Errors,* Dromio of Syracuse tells Adriana his master is in the custody of a "devil in an everlasting garment . . . a fellow all in buff."

Buff also denotes the dull, whitish yellow colour of the animal skin, and since this was also the hue of the hides of most Englishmen, the phrase *in the buff* became synonymous with nude, naked, "in the altogether," *in puris naturalibus,* and starkers.

A *buff,* as in enthusiast, was originally somebody who got thrills by watching firefighters at work, taking the nickname from the buff-coloured uniforms worn by early volunteer firemen in New York City. Today a *buff* is any aficionado, even one who is titillated by colour photos of buxom women in the buff.

If anyone's curious, the word *bumf* is short for the rather impolite *bum-fodder,* or toilet paper. Sometimes spelt *bumph,* it now means useless information.

Ever wonder why an unassuming back alley is sometimes referred to as a mews? The origins of the term have a lot to do with hawks whose feathers are falling out. Not to mention horses.

Musings on the birth of the mews

In a southern Ontario town called Toronto, there's a thoroughfare, more like a paved lane, running south from Bloor Street, just west of Spadina Avenue. It's called Sussex Mews. Curious to learn what distinguishes a mews from a plain old street, avenue, or road, I recently rode shanks' mare down the entire two-block length of this artery.

Upper Sussex Mews is flanked on one side by the blank posterior of the Jewish Community Centre of Toronto, and on the other by what appears to be the parking lot for a coin laundry establishment, bearing a huge sign advising NO PARKING AT ANY TIME. Sundry other parking/no-parking areas lead to the University of Toronto's Aura Lee Playing Field where, this noon-hour, a dozen youths savaged a soccer ball, heedless of a small sign warning that the greensward had recently been doused with a user-hostile herbicide.

Beyond the Aura Lee lea is a skating rink with pistachio green boards, but no ice. I put this down to the fact that it was August, but this by no means served to explain its neighbour across the way, a tennis court with no net. Given Toronto's weather this summer, perhaps the missing ice was more to be marvelled at.

Lower Sussex Mews, a tributary of Harbord Street, is less of the same—parking spaces, aging garages sporting aging graffiti, and one numbered building that looks as though it may well be a human habitat. The long and short of it, mostly short, is that Sussex Mews is different from a street or avenue or road, or even a crescent or court, only in that it is a fairly banal back alley.

I had hoped against hope to find a stable, or at least some vestige of erstwhile equine activity. In a phantasmagorical flight of fancy, I had even imagined happening upon a frowzled falcon or two. These seemingly eccentric chimera were not entirely footless, even if they were bootless.

In the beginning there were two kinds of *mews*, both ornithological. One was the common sea-gull that got its name from an old German word, *maiwa*. This is not the one we're interested in here (assuming, perhaps naively, that any interest exists).

The other *mew* was not a bird, but a bird-cage—specifically for hawks that were *mewing*. The verb to *mew*, or moult, was fashioned on the French *muer*, to shed feathers or horns (the latter in the case of deer, etc., not birds), which in turn was rooted in the Latin *mutare*, to change.

The *Book of St. Albans* (or the *Bokys of Hawkyng, and Huntyng*) compiled by Dame Julians Barnes in 1486, explains it pretty clearly: "Iff an hawke be in mewe, that same sercell feder [feather] shall be the last feder that she will cast, and tyll that be cast, she is never mewed." Well, maybe not all that clearly.

In any case, the verb *mew,* moult, also became the verb *mew,* to shut the bird up in a special coop for the purpose of moulting. This second verb, if nothing else, saved a lot of syllables. It also became a noun denoting the cage itself, or the act of encaging for the aforementioned purpose. Eventually the meaning extended to mean any place of confinement, and then a hiding place or den.

All well and good, you whinny, but what about the horses?

The horsey association is quite accidental. At one time, the royal hawks were mewed at London's Charing Cross. When, some time before the 15th century, the royal stables were built on the site, people continued to refer to them as The Mews. By the 17th century, *mews* was the common word for stables grouped round an open yard or alley. In another 200 years, the word meant private housing converted from stables, and today you might see it applied to brand new subdivisions or condos without a whiff of whilom gee-gee about them.

The other meaning of *mew*, of course, is the sound a cat makes. Maybe that's where this back alley called Sussex Mews got its name. But on that sunny August day, there wasn't so much as a purr. I spied no deciduous plumage, and heard nary a neigh-sayer.

"Potpourri" used to be a Spanish dish of boiled meat, "hodgepodge" was a mutton stew, and a "muddle" was a kind of American chowder. What it all boils down to is a bit of a mess.

When the meaning goes to pot

If words had publicity agents, image-polishers, spin doctors, or whatever the latest buzz is for such artificers, it would be tempting to imagine that *potpourri* had availed itself of the best in the business.

The word has nothing but pleasant connotations. It calls to mind the scent of lavender and rose petals. It evokes sweet strains of favourite medleys from string quartets in languid drawing rooms. At worst it's a harmless heterogeneity–a hodgepodge of this, that, and often the other.

Potpourri was recently blazoned (as two separate words) at the top of *The Globe and Mail's* Design page, over a story about cultivating things in large earthen pots. The heading was, I believe, a pun, but the context was in keeping with the word's generally felicitous modern meanings.

Potpourri wasn't always so redolently agreeable. It started out in Spanish as *olla podrida*, literally "putrid pot." Lexicographer Randle Cotgrave defined it in 1611 as "a Spanish dish of many severall meates boyled, or stued together." Maybe he meant glewed. The French borrowed from their neighbours and translated it to *pot pourri* (from Latin *putere*, "to be rotten"). Then the English appropriated it, *sans* translation, although the two words began to be run together as early as the mid-1770s.

At first it was a culinary term in English, as it was across the channel. But by the early 18th century, it more commonly described an aromatic mixture of dried flower petals mixed with spices in a jar. This was an image reversal unmatched in the annals of PR-dom.

Potpourri is not by any means the only word to make the transition from stew-pot to general conglomeration, although it seems to have ameliorated more than most in the metamorphosis.

An early synonym was *hotch-potch,* a rhyming version of *hotch-pot,* from the French *hocher,* to shake together. This was a mere mutton stew, except for a period in the late Middle Ages when it was a law term for a blending of properties so as to re-divide them equally among heirs. *Hotch-potch* and its modern variant *hodgepodge* now represent a "confused assemblage, a farrago."

The Latin *farrago*, "cattle fodder," came into English with that meaning, then broadened into a mixture of persons or things. The Latin word for mix, *miscere*, had an off-shoot, *miscellanea*, which meant a "hash of broken meat." From that we got *miscellany*, which can be a hash of anything.

Hash is from French *hache* (from which we also got *hatchet*), and once denoted a dish of chopped meat warmed up with gravy. Now when we "make a hash of something," it's not usually food, but just a run-of-the-mill mish-mash.

Mish-mash is a reduplication of *mash,* which in Old English was *masc,* meaning crushed grapes for making wine. Later it signified any livestock food, and by the 16th century, it also stood for any old muddle. *Muddle* as a verb originally meant to get yourself or someone else muddy. But in 1890, W.D. Whitney's *Century Dictionary in the*

U.S. also gave it a noun definition: "a kind of chowder" or "pottle made with crackers."

An Italian word, *pasticcio* (cousin of *pasta*, or paste) was used in 18th century England for "any manner of pastie or pye," usually containing meat and macaroni. In the 19th century, English speakers Frenchified it to *pastiche*, which described either "a musical potpourri" or "a picture made of pieced-together fragments," its modern meaning.

At the up-market end of this list of food-based melange words are *salmagundi* (chopped meat, anchovies, eggs, onions, and oil), *ragout* (a highly seasoned meat stew, from *ragoûter*, "to revive the taste of "), and *gallimaufry* (a dish of hashed leftovers). All of these French loans are used figuratively for a plain old mess.

Speaking of which, our all-purpose *mess* is related to the Modern French *mets*, or food. Its earliest English sense was a serving of food, or a prepared dish of a specific kind. It also developed the meaning of a company of people regularly dining together, as in the military sense.

For a while in the 14th century, *mess* also meant "food for worms"–but that's opening another can of pottage.

PART FIVE

*

Metaphor-mosis

English is festooned with colourful, playful, expressive figures of speech. Many have long since become clichés through overuse. Some have obvious origins, but others derive from metaphors with a surprising–and sometimes shocking–past.

English abounds with expressions that cast dogs in an unfavourable light–such as "gone to the dogs," "putting on the dog," or "it's a dog's life." It's doggone unfair.

Far from the cat's meow

> It seems that life in New York City is a rat race and Paris has gone to the dogs.
>
> –Social Studies Column, *The Globe and Mail.*

An odd expression, that, "gone to the dogs." Especially in a language whose cradle is a country where creatures of the canine persuasion are treated with a deference verging on cultism.

I can vouch for this devotion. I was once standing in a crowded north London pub when I felt a sharp pain in my ankle. I soon discovered I had been bitten by a tiny Pomeranian with exceedingly large teeth. Adding insult to injury, the animal's indignant owner yapped at me for 10 minutes, while most of the crowd weighed in with muttered endorsement, because I had upset the poor beast. It was a painful lesson in just how solicitous the English can be toward their dogs.

That being the case, I've often wondered why it is that the English language and its figures of speech are, well . . . so *doggone* anti-dog. Our tongue abounds with mutt metaphors, and an astonishing number of them are invidious.

In its simplest pejorative uses, *dog* is a synonym for an extremely unattractive person or an utterly inferior product. (Sports columnist Stephen Brunt added a further colloquial twist when he described a Grey Cup half-time show as a "mutt.") But there are many more complex allegories.

If you're *putting on the dog,* you're displaying obvious pretensions to grandeur, but nobody is going to think you're *the cat's meow*–more likely, *a hot dog.* When we overindulge at a party, we blame some innocent canine, because the next morning we seek metaphorical remedy in *the hair of the dog that bit us.* If at that same party we did the old lampshade-on-the-head trick, we're bound to be in somebody's *dog house.*

The hottest, muggiest days of August are known as the *dog days.* That's when the dog star Sirius, the biggest and meanest member of the constellation *Canis Major*, rises in conjunction with the sun. It's during this period that Englishmen and their dogs reputedly go out in the midday sun–but only the dogs get called mad.

Our common speech is strewn with pejorative poochisms. In extreme fatigue, we're *dog-tired.* An ill-used book gets *dog-eared.* There is nothing *nastier than a junkyard dog,* except more recently for a pit bull. A *dog in the manger* is some meanie who doesn't want you to enjoy something even though he has no use for it himself. A *dog's dinner* is an ostentatious show, while a *dog's breakfast* is–not to be too dogmatic about it–a real mess.

Still on the subject of food, English sailors in the early 19th century had a word for a singularly unappetizing meal made of dried pease boiled in a cloth; it was *dogsbody.* A century later this word came to be applied to a junior drudge who was assigned the most menial tasks.

What's another name for harass or torment? *Hound.* When we feel like complaining, what do we do? We *bitch.* And what do we call the most ruthless sort of competition? *Dog-eat-dog.*

A healthy scepticism is an acceptable, even advisable, attitude in modern society. But nobody has ever liked a cynic, except for a group of 4th century B.C. Greeks who made a philosophy out of suspecting wrong in everybody. They were called *Cynics* (from the Greek *kunicos* for doglike or currish) because they personified a dog's putative habit of sniffing suspiciously at anything or anyone new.

Other supposed canine attributes are applied to human behaviour that is less than commendable. If we appear shamefaced, downcast, guilty, or intimidated, we have a *hang-dog look.* To show true cowardice, we *run off like a dog with its tail between its legs.*

Well, *every dog has its day.* But, unlike a cat, it has only one life–and *it's a dog's life* throughout. Then it dies. Like a dog.

Strange, isn't it, that English has so many expressions involving dogs, and very few of them are complimentary. Why do we insist on calling them our best friends? I've been *worrying at this bone* for years.

But maybe I'm *barking up the wrong tree.* Mindful of that pub experience, I should probably *let sleeping dogs lie.*

With the baseball season ready to get under way, it's as good a time as any to look at all the terms from the ball-playing lexicon that have entered our everyday language.

A case of talking a good game

Well, here we are *on deck* for a whole new ball game—162 of them, in fact. So what better time to look at how the rhetoric of rounders has infiltrated our everyday language?

Let me say, *right off the bat,* that I'm not going to be giving any *Bronx cheers* to the fatuous flakes who *call 'em as they see 'em* from the broadcast booth. I'll *take a rain check* on panning the play-by-play pomposities and platitudes.

Baseball has given us many metaphors and clichés. So let's just *bat around* a few of the summer-game tropes that pepper our tongue, whether we're dyed-in-the-flannel fanatics or *out in left field.* Hang in there, even if you don't know home plate from a hole in the ground. Just keep your *eye on the ball,* the bat, and whatever else comes up.

Let's say your company's *pitching* for a major-league contract, and your sales skipper has made you the *designated hitter.* You were a *natural* to *get the nod* as a *starter* because you've been *batting .1000* since that *spring training* session you had at Banff. That's only *fair ball.*

The *scouting report* tells you that your competitor for the job isn't a *heavy hitter.* Well, *all-star* or not, he wouldn't even be in *the starting nine* if he didn't have *something on the ball.* Either that, or *a lot of clout.* Just to *play it safe,* you go over the *ground rules* in your mind. You decide you're going to have to *play hard-ball,* or you're never going to *get to first base.*

At an earlier meeting–the first of three scheduled on this *road trip*–they threw the *high, hard ones,* and you got *caught off base* a couple of times. So there are already *two strikes against you,* but you know it's only *one down and two to go.*

The second two meetings are unexpectedly scheduled for the same day, making it a *doubleheader.* What's worse, it's in the competition's *friendly confines.* This *change-up* in the plans comes right *out of left field,* but you're ready to *play ball,* even if it is *catch-up.*

When you arrive at the meeting, you discover that the *home team* has pulled a *line-up change.* The *southpaw* you expected to face has been *benched,* or *sent to the showers,* or maybe even *down to the minors. Pinch-hitting* for him is a *switch-hitter* called up from *a farm team.* This *throws a curve at you,* but you're determined not to *choke up.* You tell yourself that this guy's not even *in the same league* with you. A pleasant enough fellow, it seems, but you are comforted by the knowledge that *nice guys finish last.*

You toss some light banter back and forth during the *warmup.* Then the meeting starts, and the *rookie leads off.* He throws out a few *ball-park figures, touches all the bases,* and *gets ahead in the count.* Then, with the momentum going for him, he indulges in some *bush-league hot-dogging.* That kind of *grandstanding,* you're sure, can only lead to a *strike-out.* But that's a *judgment call.*

Just then you notice something that makes you feel like the victim of a *hit-and-run.* The rookie is a dead ringer . . . whoops, that's a whole 'nother game . . . The rookie bears a striking resemblance to the client he's *making his pitch to.* Curly blond hair, blue eyes, bull neck, cleft chin. Except for about 25 years difference in age, they look enough alike to be Minnesota twins. When the rookie inadvertently refers to the man as "Uncle Norm," you know you're caught in a *squeeze play.*

You haven't *had your innings* yet, but you know you're not even *in the ball park.* Maybe *it ain't over 'til it's over,* as the philosopher said. Maybe the fat lady hasn't sung yet. But if you're *reading the signals* right, that rookie's *rounding third and heading for home.*

You've got nobody to *go to bat* for you, and no *bullpen relief* or *bench strength.* Oh well, you think to yourself, *there goes the ball game,* and maybe the season too. You pack your briefcase and walk from the room muttering, "Wait 'til next year."

The sports world has given any number of expressions to everyday English. But do you know the sporty origins of such words as "arena" and "desultory"? The ball's in your court.

*

Why moving the goal posts isn't cricket

It's that time of year again for sports freaks, when winter games slop over into spring and spring stubs its toe on summer and summer trips over fall. It's a sportsfantasmagoria. You name the game–from bocce to beach volleyball, from mahjong to mumblety-peg, even un-NHL hockey–it's being played somewhere right now, and probably in front of a television camera.

It's too early to do any serious time-wasting, like gardening, painting, or fence-mending, so why not just sit back and let the clichés wash over you. Between periods, innings, rounds, frames, ends, sets, or chukkers, you might also reflect on the huge amount of sports jargon that has enriched or debased our language.

In "A case of talking a good game," we lobbed around some baseball lingo, but in any arena, sporting or otherwise, *a level playing field* is desirable. When *the ball's in your court*, it's important not to *drop your guard*, or *zig when you should have zagged*, no matter how good your *track record* is. If someone *moves the goal posts*, well, that's just *not cricket*.

Many gamy terms have been around so long, their origins are forgotten.

Take *arena*. It's Latin for "sand" and originally wasn't a structure but the central combat surface of a Roman amphitheatre. This area was covered with sand to absorb the blood of the wounded or slain "games" participants. Talk about the agony of defeat! (or "de feet," as de marathoner said).

Agony is from the Greek *agones* for public games. The meaning expanded to include any contest or struggle, then transferred from a physical to a mental sense. It had this sense of mental anguish when it was imported into English in the 14th century. Within two centuries it had shifted, in somewhat desultory fashion, back to a predominantly physical connotation, which it retains.

Desultory also has its roots in ancient sport. It's from the Latin *saltare*, to leap, and in the Roman Circus Maximus, a *desultor* was a performer who leapt from the back of one galloping horse to another. You don't hear the noun much any more, but the adjective survives to denote any purposeless, restless lurching from one thing to another.

What's a *lurch*? And why is it bad to be left in one? The expression *left in the lurch* is still used in cribbage and whist to describe a player who's been "skunked" or otherwise badly beaten. It was borrowed from *lourche*, a backgammon-like game that was popular in 16th century France. Now, through the magic of metaphor, we play fast and loose with its original meaning, using it to describe any situation in which someone is put in a position of unexpected difficulties.

Fast and loose was the name of a 16th century scam (or "cheating game") played on bumpkins by sharpers at country fairs and markets. The rubes were persuaded to bet they could pass a rod through some cunningly arranged loops of a belt, so that the rod would be held fast. It usually wasn't, although the con man might throw in the occasional miscue just to keep the clients interested.

There's no mistaking the sporting origin of *miscue*,

but it might not be so well known that the loan-word *debut* also made its first appearance in billiards (from French *débuter*, to make the first stroke). It came into English in the early 18th century to signify the first appearance of a stage performer, but soon was being used to describe any "coming out," particularly that of a young *debutante*.

When a handsome buck fell *head over heels* for such a belle, he was metaphorically imitating gymnasts or tumblers–although, when the figurative use came into fashion in the 14th century, it was, more logically, *heels over head*.

That young buck is, of course, a metaphor for a male beast. So why–or, more to the point, how–do we *pass the buck*? Here, the word is an abbreviation of buckhorn-handled knife. Each time the cards passed to a new dealer in poker games (probably stags), the knife was also passed on, which tended to give the dealer the upper hand in more ways than one.

And with that, the buck–and this discussion–stops here.

Using popularized technicalities may take one far from the original meaning of words and expressions. And common English abounds with words ripe for metamorphosis.

It isn't déjà vu all over again

I used to get apoplectic with puristic pique whenever I encountered what I pedantically considered a misuse of the borrowed expression *déjà vu*.

At the first hint of a prolonged losing streak by the Maple Leafs (a Toronto hockey team), the sports writers pass on to us their feeling of *déjà vu*. When the plot of a new novel bears a resemblance to an earlier work, the critics moan to us about their depressing sense of *déjà vu* (although *déjà lu* would be less inappropriate).

"Dammit," I would exclaim to myself, "don't they realize *déjà vu* has a precise meaning: the fleeting and illusory sensation of having experienced something that is, in fact, occurring or is about to occur for the first time? It is NOT history repeating itself."

It was probably the inherent burden of exclaiming such a protracted exclamation that brought on the imagined apoplexy. But at some point I realized that by "getting apoplectic," I was indulging in exactly the same sort of solecism. Apoplexy, after all, is a paralysing stroke brought on by an acute vascular lesion of the brain, or a haemorrhage–a stronger reaction than I had in mind.

What we were doing, those *déjà vu*-ers and I with my

sub-apoplectic tantrum, was using what usage guru H.W. Fowler termed "popularized technicalities."

Common English abounds with words and expressions appropriated from professions, trades, and other special pursuits. Some, like *chronic*, survive popularization with their meanings intact. But in most cases, the process drastically reduces the strength of the original word or expression–and often changes it altogether.

An *acid test* used to involve applying some nitric acid to a metallic hunk. If it survived unscathed, it was gold. Its metaphorical use as a crucial, incontestable proof was popularized by U.S. president Woodrow Wilson in 1918, when he said: "The treatment accorded Russia by her sister nations in the months to come will be the acid test of their good will."

By 1926 the figurative *acid test* was so overused that it headed Fowler's list of "hackneyed phrases." Lately, however, it seems to be giving ground to the flimsier *litmus test*, as in "Unity Talks Face Litmus Test."

If anyone stumbles on a correct use of *begging the question*, I'd be happy to hear about it. This expression, from the discipline of logic, does not (or did not) mean merely raising or suggesting or prompting a query. In fact, it had nothing to do with interrogatives. To *beg the question* (from the Latin *petitio principii*) means to base a conclusion on a premise that's just as debatable as the conclusion. It's sometimes called circular argument.

Which leads us to *leading question*. This loan from the legal world is commonly used to describe a hostile, pointed, or tricky query designed to embarrass or trap one. In fact, it's quite the opposite, a friendly question. When a lawyer tries to help his or her own witness to the desired answer, that's a leading question.

Not long ago, writer Don Gillmor used another word that has undergone a thorough transformation at the hands of the hoi polloi. "The variety show often fares better as *nostalgia* than entertainment," he said.

This conforms to the modern notion of *nostalgia*—a warm fondness for anything old and comfortable, such as fifties music, attic relics, and home cooking. But it doesn't conform to most dictionary definitions, which characterize *nostalgia* as homesickness, or a wistful longing for something far away or long ago, but now sadly out of reach—hardly warm or comfortable emotions. Even this sense is tempered from the original technical meaning in pathology: melancholia brought on by prolonged absence from home or country.

Whoops, there's another one. The adjective *melancholy* now conveys no more gravity than mild moroseness, slight mental depression (another weakened borrowing from psychology), or "the blues." In many modern applications, *melancholy* means only moodily pensive. Three centuries ago, however, you would have given a wide berth to people so described. They were irascible and given to sudden violence—understandable when you consider the word's Greek roots, *melanos*, black, and *chole*, gall or bile. Early medical practitioners believed that the mental state was caused by the physical condition of "black bile."

Which, I think, is about where I came in.

Some expressions are obviously anchored in a sea-going heritage, others less obviously so. By and large is of the less obvious variety, referring to the safety margin between a ship's course and the wind.

Salty words and by and large foggy phrases

Spending a week in Nova Scotia has reminded me that the English language is awash with words and expressions that smack of a sea-going heritage. Most of them easily betray their salty origins. Given the right ingredients, you could *splice the mainbrace* in the middle of the Sahara Desert–a feat that could leave you both *high and dry*, but in no doubt of the nautical association of those two phrases.

But other maritime metaphors have been around so long, and have become so assimilated into everyday language, that their pelagic past is shrouded in fog. By and large, they've undergone a sea change.

Take *by and large*. Experienced skippers would never dream of navigating while *three sheets to the wind*. Nor would they sail too close to the wind because a sudden change might cause the vessel to be *taken aback*, or turned right around. Rather, they would leave a safety margin between the ship's course and the wind–a practice known as sailing *by and large*. This also ensured that the steersman did not have *the wind taken out of his sails*, a condition that would cause them to "luff " or flop flaccidly. Avoiding this condition, by maintaining a prudent margin, was known as "keeping aluff," from which we get the standoffish expression *remaining aloof*.

To an Upper Canadian landlubber like me, the only salt associated with the word *slush* is the seasoning that's strewn on winter streets to make car bodies corrode. And *slush fund* evokes no images of masts and sails. But in the 18th and 19th centuries *slush* was a common shipboard term for the fat or grease left over from boiling meat. The cook skimmed this off and stored it in a barrel.

When it was full he sold the mess in the next port of call. The revenue was called a *slush fund*, and traditionally this was used to buy luxuries for the crew or for such extras as prizes for target-firing prowess.

Around the middle of the last century, the term began to broaden and take on pejorative meanings. Today it's a fund for political bribes or other seamy influence, or a budgetary allocation to be used for discretionary–and often clandestine–purposes. Depending on the era and place, *slush* has also meant watery food, trashy literature, nonsense, counterfeit money, a sloven, and, in U.S. slang, a trombone.

When someone mentions gulls, grebes, gannets, gallinules, godwits, and guillemots, I instantly think of surf and salt spray–don't you? But a *round robin*? The term is most commonly used today in sports tournaments in which all players or teams play each other. It can also mean a letter or other document circulated among a group for comments.

But this robin was not originally ornithological. It was an 18th century sailors' corruption of the French *ruban rond*, or round ribbon. When mutinous or even mildly malcontented crewmen wanted to convey a grievance to the captain, they signed their names on a strip of cloth joined at the ends to make a circle. This way, the captain couldn't tell who signed first, which made later reprisals difficult.

If the skipper did discover the ringleader's identity, there would, of course, be *the devil to pay*. But this once had an entirely different–and no less daunting–meaning for a seafarer.

The verb *pay* has at least three nautical meanings: to let out a rope or chain; to allow a ship to fall to leeward, or away from the wind; and to apply pitch or tar caulking to a wooden ship's seams. One of these seams, near the water line, was known as the *devil* because it was hellishly hard and dangerous to caulk. If you were faced with this task, you had *the devil to pay*. And while you were working on it, you could find yourself in that disquieting position of being *between the devil and the deep blue sea*.

If you're all at sea about the origin of any English metaphor, the odds are that it can be found in Shakespeare, the Bible, or in that vast ocean of colourful expressions that were born or bred on the briny. This isn't a *hard and fast* rule, but, by and large, it holds water.

If you're sinking in a sea of debt, it's hardly surprising. There's an undercurrent of hydrous hardship in the words we use to discuss commercial failure.

Damp squibs of the business world

Where is Noah now that we need him? With business busts booming, the economy could use some help from the resourceful old patriarch. After all, he managed to keep a limited company afloat while the rest of the world was in liquidation.

With no Noah to bail us out, maybe the best we can do is pace the poop deck and ponder the true meaning of some of the odd terminology we use in the business of mercantile delinquency.

The diluvian reference is apt. There is an undercurrent of hydrous hardship in the vocabulary we use to discuss commercial failure, especially in slang. To go bankrupt is to *sink*, to *go under, on the rocks,* or *down the drain*, to *founder*, or, in some cases of journalistic grandiloquence, to be *awash in a sea of red ink*. Even the phrase *belly up* refers to the orientation of a defunct fish.

Certain moist properties are associated with even the conventional language of failure. The verb *liquidate* comes from the Latin *liquidus*, but in only one of its seven senses does it have anything to do with literal wateriness.

The earliest recorded meaning was "to make something clear." In business, it meant to sort out accounts, sometimes through litigation. Since most business disputes involved nonpayment of something, the word soon came to denote paying off a debt. By the 19th century *liquidate* was a common legal and business term meaning not just to clearly set out a troubled company's liabilities, but also to apportion the assets among its creditors. That seems pretty cut and dried.

In stages, it came to mean to put an end to anything, then to stamp out, wipe out, and finally to kill. The last meaning gained grim currency during the early Stalin era, and the Russian word for it was *likvidírovat.*

Solvency also has fluid connotations, probably because of its kinship with *solvent*, *solution,* and *dissolve.*

But the English root word *solve* took its earliest meaning from the Latin *solvere*, to loosen or break up. In the 16th century it was used interchangeably with *absolve*, often thought of as "having your sins washed away." The meaning that stuck, though, was the idea of explaining, clearing up, answering, or resolving things, including mysteries, mathematical problems, riddles, and crossword puzzles.

From the 16th to the 19th century, to *solve* also meant to clear off or pay a debt, which made it an exact synonym for *liquidate*, and it too acquired the broader sense of *put an end to* or *settle once and for all*. Unlike *liquidate*, however, it didn't evolve all the way to *kill*–with the notorious exception of the noun form in the Nazi "final solution."

We often think of *solvents* and *solutions* as being dampish, but *solvency* is merely the ability to pay one's debts. It has nothing to do with wet, although *liquid assets* and a steady *cash flow* will certainly help keep you *afloat*–and, no doubt, in a buoyant mood.

If a creditor pulls the plug on you (amazing, isn't it?), you could find yourself in *receivership*. The buck now stops with the *receiver*–as it did in the medieval period, when the *receiver general* was the official who collected taxes and other tribute for the monarch. The custom and title survive in Canada, as you are reminded each time you make out a cheque to the federal government.

Why the word *receiver* was extended in the 18th century to include someone charged with administering the assets of an insolvent is not clear. But it may be worth mentioning–just to keep the liquid allegory going–that, even earlier, a person appointed to take control of a shipwreck was called the Receiver of Wrecks. Here too, Canada still has such an office, and the duties have expanded to include crashed airplanes.

The last resort of the fiscally flattened is *bankruptcy*. This comes from the Italian *banca rotta*, or "broken bench," after the medieval custom of fracturing a welshing money-changer's bench, rather than his kneecaps, which is today's custom. The Italian *rotta* (from Latin *ruptus,* "break," which eventually gave our *bankrupt* its second syllable) also means "wrecked" as in shipwreck.

Just remember all this next time you're tempted to go in over your head.

A reference to the Constitution as a cat's cradle leads to reflections on the origin of that phrase–and where did the expressions "pussyfooting" and "cat's paw" come from?

When the cat's got your tongue

The national unity agreement got called many things. In one huge headline it was called the "Cat's cradle constitution," and that just naturally roused my curiosity.

Is a cat's cradle anything like a dog's breakfast? Or a mare's nest? A can of worms? A mess of verbiage?

No, it's a game in which you form a symmetrical pattern with string on your fingers. Another person removes the loops so as to form another pattern, and so on alternately. Used as an attributive noun before "constitution" it signified complicated, intricate, tortuous, and maybe even loopy. Perhaps that's because the origin of *cat's cradle*–like the origin of the word *cat* and of the animal itself–is a mystery.

Some word sleuths believe *cat's cradle* began as *cratch-cradle*. A *cratch* is a rack or manger for holding livestock fodder. In Middle English it was *crecche*, from the French *crèche*, or crib, and it may be that the string pattern resembled this structure. There is also the suggestion of a folkloric connection with the manger of the Nativity.

The medieval verb *cratch*, to snatch or grab at, as with claws, could provide another clue. It could fairly describe the action of a child eagerly or clumsily removing the string from another's fingers.

According to both theories, *cratch* evolved through folk etymology—that quaint process by which an obsolete word is replaced over time with a similar-sounding, familiar one—into *cat's*. But the *Oxford English Dictionary* gets its back up about these theories, saying they are "not founded on facts."

Founding facts are also scarce for the word *cat* itself. The classic words were Latin *felis* and Greek *ailouros* (from which we formed the word *ailurophobia* for "morbid fear of cats"). But, around 2,000 years ago, the word *gata* began showing up in Greek, and *catta* in Latin. Nobody knows whence these obviously related words came, but in one similar form or another they represent *cat* in virtually every European language today.

The affectionate name *puss* is also of unknown derivation. The *OED* speculates that it originally was merely the sound made by humans in calling a cat.

All this inscrutability seems apt for a creature that has inspired fascination, fear, and even idolatry in humans for eons. Cats, which share one of every two households in Canada, are the subject of untold proverbs, legends, superstitions, and metaphors. The Romans used to say, "*Dum felis dormit, mus gaudet et exsilit antro*," or "when the cat's asleep, the mouse rejoices and leaps from its hole." Not quite as rhythmic as the modern English version, but it's the same idea.

There are dozens of cat-mentions in Shakespeare. When Lady Macbeth chides her hesitant husband for acting like the "poor cat i' th' adage" she's referring to a proverb that first appeared in English print around 1225: "*Cat lufat visch, ac he nele his feth wete*," which translates to "a cat loves fish, but doesn't like to get his feet wet." Maybe this is where *pussyfooting* began.

And that's a short step to *cat's paw*. It derives from a fable in which a monkey used his feline friend's foot to drag hot chestnuts from the fire. Today it figuratively describes a willing human tool, or a dupe. In nautical parlance it also denotes a pattern caused by a light breeze on water, or a twisted knot in a rope.

Other anatomical parts figure in cat-lore. *Cat's eyes* may be gems or highway reflectors that resemble the animal's noctilucent orbs. The *cat-o'-nine-tails*, a cruel whip with nine knotted flails, was once an official penal instrument. The *cat's whiskers* (or *pyjamas*, or *meow*) is quite the opposite of *something the cat dragged in*.

We've only scratched the surface of the subject. But one prominent pussophile, T.S. Eliot, cut to the heart of the matter with *Old Possum's Book of Practical Cats*, on which the modern musical was based. In "The Addressing of Cats," he offered this comparison, by way of profound insight: "A dog is a dog–but A CAT IS A CAT."

PART SIX

*

Fouler Modern English Usage

From sports commentators, advertisers, the press, politicians, and protectors of political correctitude; from lotus-eaters and from well-meaning but misguided pedants, the language is under a state of constant siege. Nevertheless, it's holding strong.

A perusal of a local "new life monthly" reveals all sorts of information about alembics, self-affirmation, and the like. Trouble is, none of it's comprehensible.

Please don't pass the gestalt

The first thing about *Dimensions*–"Toronto's New Life Monthly"–that caught my eye was the line that ran clear across the top of the front page. It read: "COMPLIMENTARY COPY COMPLIMENTARY COPY FREE COPY FREE COPY $2.50."

Being as canny a Caledonian-Canadian as the next, I instantly grasped that the publisher's instincts ran more strongly–by a 4-1 margin, in fact–toward giving the paper away than charging for it. I therefore hastily grabbed a copy and slunk away to a park bench where, in the company of five squirrels whose symbolism would soon become clear, I entered a new dimension of light reading.

The second thing that caught my eye, in spite of some rather risqué behaviour by two of said squirrels, was that the contents of *Dimensions* were just as arcane, to put it charitably, as the cover proclamation re price/no price.

Take the Publisher's Letter. After he got warmed up to his subject (the identification of which still eludes me), he enthused: "For this issue of *Dimensions* we went out and asked a number of individuals, active in the new consciousness, to talk/write about how 'the shadow' shows itself in their lives and work."

Now, maybe *Dimensions'* regular readers know what "the shadow" is (it does not seem to refer to a radio character of the 1940s), but this casual peruser was left in a profound umbra. It was of little avail to turn to the talking/writing of some of those individuals, whose new-consciousness workouts were so rudely interrupted by the publisher's inquisitiveness. Each of the 14 (including Ace Osmer, editor/writer, and a person called Oriah Mountain Dreamer) had a quite distinct definition of "the shadow," and none of them was excessively burdened by comprehensibility.

Michael Owen, Jungian psychotherapist, was one of those canvassed. "The least accessible shadow," he talked/wrote, "only emerges after a prolonged effort at viewing oneself from the perspective of the Self. It is not the personal or collective shadows that are dispelled by affirmations or come at the bidding of a growth workshop–it has nothing to do with personal history, it cannot be primalled, gestalted, rolfed or analysed away."

Kathryn Gill, identified as a Bodymind Integrative Therapist, came closest to striking a responsive chord in this aching lump of flesh and bone. "My shadow," she confessed, "manifests itself in somatic symptoms. I've developed a metabolic disturbance and a mild arthritic condition." Could this, I idly speculated, be the long-sought key to my ingrown toenail?

Perhaps Ms. Gill should matronize one of *Dimensions'* many advertisers of esoteric services, emollients, and other balmy products. How about Janet and Stewart Farrar, "the internationally famous British witches/authors"? Or Tifrah Q. Warren, Ph.D., who offered counselling in an ad rather off-puttingly entitled "Welcome To Yourself."

There was Tamara Penn, "Professional Rebirther," and Marie Ripley, whose blurb (believe it or not) invited the reader to "join with me in truth and light as I merge with my High Self to bring you insight and guidance. Consciousness Channelling. $65 for 45 minutes (includes taped cassette)."

For a fun time, how about Mama Afrika Goddess, whose ad urged me to follow the beat that is "calling you to African goddess dance and therapy." Then again, if you believe money is the root of all shadows, you could visit Heather Skelton, B.Sc., who described herself as a Financial Wellness Consultant and Income Tax Minimizer.

Not all was doom and gloom in this periodical netherworld. Getting back to the Publisher's Letter, we read that "the answer to the question of the shadow will determine the future of humanity and the biosphere. A new kind of human being is gestating [and maybe *gestalting*] and struggling to be born amid the chaos of our time . . . Millions of human beings are responding to a worldwide evolutionary pulse beating every day more strongly in the heart of humanity."

And if that doesn't make you feel a holistically lot better, let's fast-forward to the tail-end of an interview conducted by the peripatetic publisher with Dr. Jean Houston, director of the Foundation for Mind Research:

> Pub: Do you have those experiences where on a particular day you wake up, you feel peculiarly energized, something seems to be grinding inside you, something is moving . . .
> J.H.: Oh yes, yes.
> Pub: . . . you turn on the television and a volcano just erupted.
> J.H.: It's like catching an evolutionary vibration and being a distillation chamber, an alchemical alembic for the world soul.
>
> Continued next issue . . .

I think I'll skip the next issue. Complimentary or not, it's too much for me.

In the blitzkrieg on "objectionable" language, it's impossible for an innocent bystander to keep track of which terms are in and which are out.

*

Casualties of the verbal wars

The perversion of language for personal, political, or merely pansophistic purposes is nothing new. Despots of every stripe, zealots of every *ology* and *ism* in every generation from the beginning of time, all the windbags, bullies, satraps, snake-oil salesmen, propagandists, and proselytizers in history–even some earnest altruists–have tried to capture hearts and minds by first manipulating words.

Truth is not the first casualty of war. Words are. Whether it's a shooting war or a struggle for intellectual dominion, the first order of business is to round up time-honoured words, strip them of integrity, dress them in uniforms of deceit, and send them on carpet-bombing missions in support of some meretricious objective or other.

The technique was starkly synthesized by Orwell's Big Brother. His equating of polar opposites–"War is Peace," "Love is Hate"–represented the ultimate degradation of words in a hateful cause.

Somewhere on the inconsequential, but nevertheless noteworthy, end of the scale lie the attempts by well-meaning but often myopic activists involved in current causes that range from genuine to merely popular.

Their offence is usually little more than the employment of euphemism, those verbal fig leaves that disguise meaning and inhibit clear communication.

Several years ago the Metropolitan Toronto Association for Retarded Children, in an apparent attempt to discourage pejorative labelling, changed the last two words to "Community Living." This will probably achieve one objective (no mindless bigot is likely to mock a child with the epithet "community liver") but will anyone but insiders ever know just what the renamed association stands for?

In the welter of language revisionism being generated by those in the vanguard of opposition to such things as sexism, racism, ableism, ageism, speciesism (discriminating against nonhuman animals) and–a new one to me–resourcism (abusing nature), it's impossible for a sensitive average person to keep track of which terminology is in and which is out. It's hard to be politically or socially correct when the glossary of terms goes out of date every fortnight or so.

It's even difficult for people within the same passionate cause. Mark Meisner, a graduate student in environmental studies at York University, makes the point plaintively in an article in the summer issue of *Probe Post*, the magazine of the Pollution Probe Foundation.

Mr. Meisner urges caution bordering on cynicism toward erstwhile favoured expressions such as "green," "environmentally friendly," and even "environmentalist," arguing quite rightly that they have been co-opted by many whose motives may be suspect.

But he goes well beyond that. We must, he says, purge our language of such expressions as "political *wilderness*," "not out of the *woods* yet," and "concrete *jungle*" because they place a negative value on natural things. We must also get rid of "animal insults" such as "greedy as a pig" and "snake in the grass," he says. Those on the far fringe of "speciesism" want to replace the word *pet* with *animal companion* and so eradicate the arrogant human notion of animal ownership.

When *isms* meet or clash, the situation can become even more confounding. Feminists and environmentalists alike decry female stereotyping of the natural world, as in the expressions "virgin land" and "the rape of Nature." Even the name *Mother Nature* has to go, according to eco-feminist Elizabeth Dodson Gray, lest we delude ourselves into thinking that no matter how we abuse her, she will forgive us and provide for us–an obviously "human-centred conceit," with the emphasis on the second syllable of *human*.

Probe Post unwittingly proves the point that extremes and contradictions are the shrapnel in the war of words. While Meisner inveighs against regarding nature's bounty as "resources" and proscribes the use of possessive pronouns with natural things, a full-page ad in the magazine is headed: "Soil–Our Vanishing Resource."

Similarly, while Mr. Meisner warns that almost anything labelled "green" these days should be black-listed, the magazine carries an ad for something called "The Green List," another for "The Canadian Green Consumer's Guide" (which also mentions "pets"), and a story entitled "Green Cops To The Rescue." There is also a proprietary reference to "our planet," a laudatory article about an extremist group whose credo is "No Compromise in Defence of Mother Earth," and a bunch of other words that don't meet Meisner's demanding standards of acceptability.

War may be hell, as that consummate practitioner William Tecumseh Sherman said. But ideological combat can be devilish too, especially on innocent words that get caught in the crossfire.

It's always instructive—and fun—to listen to sportscasters on TV. How else would you hear of an "uphill swim" or a goalie with the "sword of Damascus" hanging over his head?

*

Manglings of the jock-jabberers

Wrong, wrong, wrong.

Columnist Rick Salutin got it wrong when he criticized sportscasters for their "solemn and pompous" masculine pontification.

Letter-to-the-editor writer C.G. Sumner got it wrong when he castigated jock-talkers for poisoning the English language and setting a bad example for youngsters.

Television critics get it wrong all the time when they run their remote controls ragged in a futile search for conventional laughs.

Lemme tellya this: Virtually the only yuk-yuks to be found in the otherwise vast comedic wasteland of television are the audio portions of sporting events. Mr. Salutin quite misguidedly says he has "taken to sometimes watching sports events with the mute on." Well, call me an eccentric couch potato, but I've taken to only listening to sports telecasts. There are only so many thrilling "big-play" variations in any game, but the English language's line-up of more than half-a-million words gives jock-jabberers an infinity of possibilities for mirthful mangling. Even if they only play them one word at a time.

"Saskatchewan has won one game in a row," one breathless common-tater said recently. Even that modest streak might have been the envy of the Edmonton Eskimos one Sunday this fall. "For Edmonton," the broadcaster said, "it's been an uphill swim all afternoon." And for exasperated, ersatz Inuits, even that tough sledding was preferable to the plight of the hockey goalie who, I heard, had "the sword of Damascus hanging over his head." If he'd been a football player, he could have tried a conversion on the road to Damocles.

Some jocks have a knack of getting right to the pith of the matter. A comparatively articulate Blue Jay was the subject of a pregame interview, alternately rolling his eyes and furrowing his brow in concentration as a "colour commentator" reeled off a series of rhetorical questions about the team's poor performance. It was a lot to absorb, but the player cogently summed up: "You're correctly right there, Fergie."

Another agreeable sort, commenting on a particularly platitudinous observation by his mike-mate, said: "That's certainly a truism, Frank."

Most broadcast teams have at least one former player on their roster, and this gives us a special insight into the proceedings. One-time quarterback Terry Bradshaw explained why coaches and players don't publicly discuss the extent of injuries: "You can't let anyone know you've got a kink in your armour."

A superannuated soccer star offered this biologically intriguing assessment of a participant: "If he had Catliff's left foot and Mobilio's left foot, he'd be quite a player." Not much of a dancer, I'll wager, but he might have elicited this comment of another sportscaster after a splendid play in an otherwise inept game: "That's an incongruity!"

Consistency is important, right? So the audience for a recent U.S. college game was relieved to hear that, while Syracuse had hired a new coach, "the continuity continued on." Syracuse was likely taking a leaf from the playbook of another team that, despite "player-personnel" changes, was able to "keep the momentum moving forward."

In the world of sports–which, as one announcer reminded us, is just a "microscosm" of the real world–things can get pretty complex. Witness how Calgary Stampeder coach Wally Buono described the task of defending against the elusive British Columbia quarterback Doug Flutie: "To try and stop him is impossible. But to try to limit the fact that he's so good after the fact is something you can do by contain and pressure." And you wondered why you have to have a college degree to play this game?

Some jocksters go to great lengths to elucidate. "That's Toronto's last time-out," said one recently. Then, lest anyone should miss the subtlety of the issue, he elaborated, "They are finished having any time-outs left." Another, obviously giving 110 per cent, managed to work three grammatical tenses into one profound philosophical synthesis: "The future for Western is right now, or else they're history."

No one sport dominates in the rib-tickling department. An announcer in the racquets racket intoned that failing to practise diligently "is a death knoll for a tennis player"–presumably sending him to the scrap-heap. A golf gasser described a green as being "surrounded by water on three sides."

So lighten up, guys. Sports are not only fun but funny. Listen harder, watch less, and you may find that this dud's for you.

There's nothing like an election
to make the press shovel out the clichés–
landslides, slugfests, winds of change, new brooms.
Everything but the kitchen sink.

A vote against enfeebled phrases

It wasn't just another day in Ontario. It was a day that will live in infamy, or maybe ignominy, if what I read in the papers was true.

There were *landslides* in Sault Ste. Marie, Kingston, Brockville, and at least six other cities. There were *avalanches* in three more, while in assorted towns, villages, townships, and regional municipalities there were *dogfights, slugfests, toe-to-toe battles,* and, as Tuesday evening wore on, quite a number of *cliffhangers.* In one city, not known for quirky meteorological happenings, four people were *blown out* of their offices by *winds of change.*

Pillars of civic society all over Ontario were *beaten, crushed, trounced, thumped, skunked, bounced, booted, turfed out,* and *sent packing.* Some were *swept in* on *waves* of public concern, but as many others were *swept out* by *new brooms.* In one instance, an erstwhile respected member of the community–people had called him "Your Worship"–was given a *very rude awakening,* and several others of equally high repute were evidently seen *hanging on by the seat of their pants.* Would you believe that London's board of control *underwent a facelift?*

Yes, it was municipal election day in the province of the trillium and trite electoral reportage.

I can only surmise that reporters and editors were so besotted by banal bombast, orotund oratory, and sundry campaign cant and claptrap that they could report the polling results only in the hackneyed terms with which they had become imbued.

Clichés, in other words, were running amok, like chickens with their heads cut off, or bulls in a china shop. And when clichés abound, there is fun to be found.

Consider, for example, the task facing June Rowlands, Toronto's first distaff chief magistrate. I read several times that *she has her job cut out for her*—a gross understatement if there ever was one. According to editorial writers and other oracles, it's imperative that she get right to work *healing wounds, mending fences, building bridges, rebuilding burnt bridges* (two clichés for the price of one!), *fostering an environment of cooperation,* and *forging a consensus.*

She must *reach out* to all the citizens while straddling both sides of a *divided council.* And all this while being hobbled by a chain of office and, at least for a while yet, *nursing her fractured ankle.*

To my—and no doubt Mayor-elect Rowlands's—immense relief, no one called on her to put her nose to the grindstone and her shoulder to the wheel, at the same time keeping her ear to the ground and a weather eye out while toeing the line. Nevertheless, I think she will need more than *a long track record of progressive Liberalism* (sic) to perform the contortions already demanded of her.

My guess is that some reporters had actually fallen asleep by the time they had to write their election stories.

"Voters in the City of York flexed their muscles last night by booting out six of the eight incumbent councillors," said one report. In a similar but less violent vein, the Guelph mayor with the felicitous name of John Counsell was "a shoe-in for re-election."

One of the lucky survivors in York was Frances Nunziata, who not only *blew the whistle* on the Fairbank Park scheme but also *scuttled* it. Then, on the day of reckoning–Terrible Tuesday–she "stood her ground against a barrage of criticism . . . and swept Ward Seven by a 10-to-1 margin."

If you didn't know, another reporter reminded you that Fairbank Park was "the catalyst that awakened" ordinary Yorkers to what was going on at City Hall.

In North York, "a grassroots citizens campaign to turf out incumbent councillors fizzled." I was okay on the cunning grassroots/turf out connection but the "fizzled" fazed me. I was also perplexed when I read that "several other races that were expected upsets did not turn out that way." Could they have been upsets if they were expected? And since they didn't, weren't they after all? Like the contest in Orangeville, where Mary Rose defeated two opponents in a "surprise turnaround"?

Before I reach out to unboot my word processor, let me give a tip of my hat–one of the few that didn't get thrown into a ring somewhere in the past two months–to the Toronto reporter who came up with the best unintentional pun of the day. He began a paragraph with this: "In other wards . . . "

It's time to look back on the year and hand out backhanders to the folks who have mangled, misused, debased, and downright done dirty to the English language.

Razzberries in season

Lay-deez and gents, y'r attention pleez (flourish of hautboys, strumpets, and symbols). Thank you. It's time for the First Annual Classic Year-End Word Play Awards Presentation. So without further adieu, here are the winners:

The Sault Ste. Marie Civic Cross de Guerre– for bilingualism above the call of duty and beyond all reason–To Dan Kepley, CBC-TV "colour commentator." He described two players, who were engaged in a shouting match (or "in each other's face," to use the tiresomely offensive vernacular) as having a "*tête*-to-*tête*." This prompted at least one viewer to fervently wish that Mr. Kepley would become *hoarse de combat*.

The Molehill-cum-Mountain Gold Medal for Gross Exaggeration–To CFTO News, whose description of Michael Jackson's new video as an epic was tantamount to calling a Bugs Bunny cartoon a saga.

The 24-Carat Iron Pyrite Paradigm Mounted on a Whoopee Cushion–To *The Globe and Mail* travel writer whose introductory paragraph was this: "What do you do when the Golden Goose decides that the comfort of the pillow upon which it lays its eggs, is not enough to justify the pain of continuous birth?" Readers who laboured painfully through that metaphorical maze discovered, somewhat anticlimatically [*sic; see page 101*], that the story was about a nose-dive in airline business-class travel.

The Dances-With-Waste Inuit Soupbone Carving with Fuchsia Leotards—To Ontario Environment Minister Ruth Grier for her bold attempt to combine recycling with physical fitness in a new program of "aerobic composting."

The "Toys R Us" Tinsel Tassel for Cavalier Use of the Alfabet—To CBC Radio's Thunder Bay operative, who in one brief report managed to hoist the "r" out of Feb_uary and plunk it into perseRvere.

The Platinum-Plated Paradox, with Curled-Lip Filigree—To *The Globe and Mail* editorial page, which began a screed with these words: "Driving one more nail into the coffin of the idea that a sovereign Quebec can have its cake and eat it too . . . " Not only did this writer mercilessly mangle two bromides, he or she made a hash of the second one in itself. It's *eat your cake and have it too.*

The Nice-Try-But-No-Cigar Manganese Medallion—To Fairweather clothier, whose ad for leather pants was headed: "At $79.99, You'll Be Suede By The Value."

The Not-Even-Close Stale Stogie for Stretching a Pun Beyond All Recognition—To Levi's, for its pre-Christmas transit ad that said simply, in big letters, "KNöW WELL." Most readers would probably have missed the point entirely if it hadn't been for the cunning use of those two little dots—even if they *were* over the "o" instead of the "e" as in *Noël.*

The Solid-Lead, Gamma-Ray-Impervious Dunce Cap for the Most Nauseating Neologism of the Year—To the copywriter who produced the ad for CBC-TV that read, in part: "With a fallout estimated to be 90 times more *impactful* than Hiroshima, the effects of Chernobyl will be felt for generations to come."

The Mixmaster Laurel Wreath on a Bed of Warped Scrabble Tiles–For the most mangled metaphor of the year, to the U.S. lawyer who said of a court's lenient treatment of President George Bush's son, Neil, for his involvement in the Savings and Loan shemozzle: "This is a slap on the wrist with a velvet hammer."

The 110-Per-Cent Pure Man-Made Onyx Oscarette–For oxymoron of the year, to another football common-tater, Joe Galat, who told Grey Cup viewers that the quarterback called a "silent audible." Let's–or let's not–hear it for Joe!

Nominations for next year's awards will open January 2. Happy New Year!

Advertisements have a nasty habit of mangling the English language. Where but in an ad would you read about brand-new "heirlooms" or "innovative lot sizes"?

Some fevered pitches

Not long ago, pedantic dudgeons soared when a distillery advertised both its product and its ignorance–or craven namby-pambyism–by saying its gin is "still *drank* the way it was 60 years ago."

Public outrage didn't quite reach the altitudes achieved four decades ago when a tobacco purveyor prompted epidemic indignation by claiming that one of its products "tastes good, like a cigarette should." Still, the lapse attracted spirited tirades in various forums.

Some felt the gin-mill's gaffe was no accident. But surely no dealer in alcoholic potables would be so prudish as to consciously vandalize the language rather than allow the dreaded word *drunk* to appear in its promotional messages. Would it?

What's more interesting to speculate on is this: Why do the part-time word-dogs feel the urge to nip at the heels and solecisms of some advertisers and not others? Maybe in the two cases in point, the combination of shoddy grammar and shady merchandise was just too much for the pure of language and sweet of breath.

Heaven knows, there are enough low, low, everyday atrocities in advertising to keep the truly dedicated nitpicker in a perpetual state of wrath–or hysteria.

The degradation of words is depressing. Birks

advertised a sterling flatware set as "*A very special gift that is actually an heirloom!*" For how many generations of which families have these "gifts" been handed down? Or are they "actually" brand-new heirlooms?

Springdale, "A New Town for a New Tomorrow," took full-page ads to offer "Founding Families" a "free grant" if they signed up to be part of this latest exurban sprawl. They also had their choice of "16 different innovative lot sizes." Now, it seems to me that housing lots come in small, medium, and big, and that none of these, or any gradations between them, can possibly be characterized as "innovative."

"It is ironic," says one car-maker, "that while most luxury sedans offer a seemingly endless array of standard amenities, they still relegate safety features like dual air bags to the options list." Says another: "Ironically the automobile with the highest resale value is also the one you'd be least likely to part with." There isn't one jot or tittle of irony in either of those situations, and I for one would be grateful if the agencies responsible would stop savaging perfectly good words like *irony* long enough to consult a dictionary to find out what they mean.

Sometimes it looks as though the copywriters simply tossed a whole bag of Scrabble tiles on the floor and printed the random result. Here's the entire text of a recent magazine ad: "It's what rewards us over time that's always best. Things constant as the certainty of black and white, or flawless as the subtle fade of indigo. Those with a presence that can frame and meld and then oblige. Simply Great Shirts. GAP." Big Gap, I'd say.

Actually, there's no certainty at all to black and white. Otherwise, there couldn't be a "whiter than white." Or a "newer than new." In the hyperbolic world of adland, superlatives and absolutes are just not good enough, although some advertisers think *penultimate* is somehow more quintessential than *ultimate*. A furniture firm is so enraptured by multisyllabic sibilance that it uproariously labels one of its high-priced lines "Antithesis." Is this the ultimate in penultimatization?

Retailers no longer have stock, goods, merchandise, or wares. They have *collections* or *systems*. Everything from clothing to cars to furniture to make-up to houses to wallpaper to toilet bowls is part of a collection. But not doors which, with their necessary hinges, handles, and locks, are now *entry systems*.

Among the other words that advertisers have pounded into meaninglessness are: quality, value, premium, luxury, exclusive, convenient, heritage–and much, much more. There are still a few words you can take literally; *incredible* and *while quantities last*, for example.

There is, happily, comic relief in the real estate ads. One offered "the renound Los Robles Estate," but didn't–thank goodness–mention how innovative the grownds were. Another described a home with a "Rousseauesque" garden, but before I could figure out whether this meant the painter or the philosopher I was distracted by the shocking news that this same house had a "lascivious master!"

It's enough to drive a person to drank.

The Globe and Mail *has put the "u" back into such words as labour and flavour. But Canadian Press has refused to let this color its judgment.*

No U-turn on "-or" spellings

There is no honour at Canadian Press. Or colour, or valour, or candour, or humour, or fervour, or even glamour. Everyone's favourite wire service has announced that–*pace Globe and Mail*–it is remaining, in its own words, "non-U."

Supervising Editor Peter Buckley, and a crew of CP stalwarts known for their rigour, if not *mortis,* laboured six months to bring out a new *CP Stylebook* to mark the national news agency's 75th anniversary. Rumour has it that the result of their endeavours was published last week, but the event was greeted by a singular lack of clamour–unlike the occasion when the *Globe* caused ecstatic outbreaks of the vapours in Loyalist parlours across the land by reverting to the *-our* spelling of such words as *arbour, dolour, tumour, saviour* and *demeanour.*

This leaves the *Globe* in isolated splendour as the only sizeable Canadian newspaper to favour the *-our* spelling, and leaves the rest of us in a state of massive confusion about what is the proper Canadian way. Contradictions and ambiguities abound, not only between the respective stylebooks of these two national institutions, but within each book itself.

Isn't it odd that the *Globe,* which is once again enamoured of the "British" *-our*, chooses as its official dictionary the American *Funk & Wagnalls Canadian*

College Dictionary, while CP, savouring the total *-or* style of our neighbours to the south, relies on the *Concise Oxford Dictionary*?

"Maintaining consistency can be troublesome," says the *CP Stylebook*. And how! On the one hand, CP opts for the American *-or*, and on the other it favours the un-American *-re* spellings in words such as *centre, theatre,* and *litre*. It embraces *program* over *programme*, but will endorse only *cheques*, not *checks*.

CP obviously harbours some discomfort about its *-or* decision. The new stylebook contains a lengthy apologia, and belabours the point even further in a "backgrounder" sent as succour to member newspapers to help them respond to "the inevitable letters about spelling that you receive."

The backgrounder correctly points out that *-our* spellings had fallen into bad odour even in England until the Yankee Noah Webster prescribed across-the-board *-or* spellings in his 1828 dictionary. This seems to have caused rancour in the Mother Country and the colonies, and galvanized resolve to preserve the few *-our* words that had survived the usage evolution. The list today comprises only 34 basic words (the gang's all here).

But CP reveals a chink in its armour when it calls in the expert witnesses. "The *Shorter Oxford Dictionary* of 1933," it says, "notes . . . that *color* has been used at times instead of *colour* in England from the 15th century." True, but the longer *Oxford English Dictionary* (2nd edition, 1989) says this: "*Colour* . . . has been the normal spelling in England from the 14th c.; but *color* has been used occasionally, chiefly under the [Latin] influence, from the 15th c., and is now the prevalent spelling in the U.S."

CP leaves the last word to "the very British and very respected Henry W. Fowler, whose *Modern English Usage* has for decades been an authority on the language." Fowler is quoted as saying that if the die-hards put "national prejudice aside" they'd find that keeping the *-our* words served no useful purpose. CP fails to point out, however, that in every individual entry for an *-our* word, Fowler says: "Keep the *-u-*."

And if CP really believes a book written in 1926 about English in England to be the last word on 1993 Canadian English usage, it should ban the words *bureaucrat, climactic, coastal, electrocute, speedometer, gullible, pacifist,* and *racial*, all of which Fowler scornfully classified as "barbarisms" or "abortions."

In any case, Fowler's book was about usage, not spelling, and when he wrote, "Keep the *-u-*," he was merely noting that this was the preponderant flavour of English spelling at that time—as it still is in Canada outside of the popular press. It's no argument to say *-or* is commonly used in Canada; it's common because CP and its members purvey it in large quantities every day.

This may be a trifling matter. But language is a keystone of culture, and a culture is distinguished by many subtle shadings of sounds, looks, and behaviour. I say, with uncontrite and *u*-ful fervour, let's keep vigour and ardour (etc.) in our English.

Everybody enjoyed his? his or her? his/her? their? meal. Why is it that a language as rich as ours has failed to come up with an answer to this tricky gender problem?

Sex and the single pronoun

WARNING

> The following contains passages dealing with explicit gender, and extreme violence to conventional wisdom. Pedantical guidance advised.

Let's delve a little deeper into the working manuals of those two great national organs (you were warned), *The Globe and Mail* and The Canadian Press. They're worth a second look for two reasons: They mirror current Canadian language habits better than any usage book available, and they influence those habits because they bear directly on much of our daily reading matter.

Despite significant differences, such as the *colour-color* dichotomy discussed earlier, both style books (or stylebooks, depending on which one you follow) reflect the broad changes taking place in our thought and language as the millennium tiptoes to a conclusion. The two have dramatically different ways of handling handles such as *Ms., Mrs.,* and *Mr.*, but, significantly, they agree that when you need a nuptials-neutral feminine title, *Ms.* will do the job. In the *Globe*'s previous book, issued in 1976, *Ms.* was barred except in stories about the title itself, and then without the period.

CP beat the *Globe* in embracing *Ms.*, but the wire service doesn't bend with every capricious zephyr of popular usage. It won't be bullied or cowed into accepting "cumbersome coinages" such as *alderperson, chairperson, salesperson,* and *spokesperson*, though for some reason it condones *newspaperwoman*, five syllables worth of cumbersomeness.

And *gender,* says CP unmincingly, is about grammar; *sex* entails males and females. The *Globe* manual, on the other hand, accepts the increasingly common–but curiously coy–practice of substituting *gender* for *sex,* and has a section headed, "Be gender-free or gender-specific."

Nowhere is semantic vexation more apparent than in the sections dealing with sex and the single pronoun (third person). Both style books, like most reference works, pussyfoot around the prickly question of which pronoun should represent an antecedent of dual or indefinite gender, as in, "Everybody enjoyed *his, his or her, his/her, their* meal." The problem exists because our language–one of the richest and most versatile on earth–inexplicably hasn't assigned an appropriate word to this task.

Both books dismiss any combination that uses the virgule, or slash. They'll accept *his or her* (but don't mention *her or his*) if necessary, and they reject *their* because it's plural and everybody knows *everybody* and similar words are singular. The *Globe*'s last-resort advice is to recast the sentence, while CP says that when all else fails, "It is proper English to let *he* (*him, his*) stand as a word of common or indeterminate gender." I hear that CP also does a passable imitation of King Canute.

Here comes the outrageous part. Why, if I may use the provocative case, do we keep insisting it's wrong to use *they, them,* or *their* in these circumstances, when all of us but the most fastidious fuss-budgets do it all the time? Here's how the *Globe* book words the taboo: "Although the pronouns *they* and *their* are increasingly heard in spoken English to refer back to a singular subject . . . avoid this usage in written form."

It's a shame, really, that this advice wasn't available to Chaucer, Shakespeare, Goldsmith, Swift, Thackeray, Fielding, Byron, Austen, Auden, Shaw, Orwell, and the translators of the Authorized Version of the Bible—all of them guilty of this supposed solecism. How did *Ms.* make it in 15 years, while after six centuries a common and consistent usage is still anathema?

No one tut-tutted until well-meaning and influential fixers started codifying grammar in the 18th century. Among the conventions they agreed on was that, in the case of mixed or uncertain gender in the antecedent, the manly pronouns should shoulder the burden. Anybody who can't guess the gender of these grammarians, please raise their hand.

The "rule" stood unchallenged until well into this century when women began to realize, and resent, the grammatical discrimination, and say, "Hey, we're part of everybody, and we're not *he's* or *hims*."

Why do we torment ourselves by clinging to this intolerable tenet? If we were so observant of other rules laid down by the 18th century linguistic lawgivers we'd still be addressing each other as *thou* and *thee*. I'd personally find that less onerous than constantly trying to write around the pronoun problem, and certainly less offensive than arrogantly and "properly" applying masculine labels to all of humankind.

Note: This column appeared on February 8, 1992. The following July, William Safire, in his "On Language" column in the Sunday *New York Times Magazine,* came to the same approving conclusion about the use of the plural pronoun with words such as "everybody" and "anybody." But neither of us can claim to be in the vanguard of this movement.

In *The Art of Plain Talk,* published in 1946, Rudolf

Flesch said: "As long as English does not do away with gender, like Hungarian, why not use *their* as a practical makeshift device where neither *his* nor *her* fits?"

He listed citations from Fielding, Roosevelt, Churchill, and Edmund Wilson to show how naturally the plural pronoun serves a singular purpose in some circumstances. "So you see that grammarians' superstitions get in the way when you try to write simple English," Flesch said. "In fact, grammar itself gets in the way."

Another eminent scholar, Otto Jespersen, reached the same conclusion even earlier. In *Language: Its Nature, Development and Origin* (1921), he wrote: "The substitution of the plural for the singular is not wholly illogical; for *everybody* is much the same thing as 'all men', and *nobody* is the negation of 'all men' . . . "

Committing such mistakes as writing "rod iron" for "wrought iron" is not the sole province of a generation of TV watchers. It's a long-standing tradition in the development of language.

*

It's still grated cabbage

Every so often the *Globe* carries an article about the hilarious mutilation of words by children. Typically, we're allowed or encouraged to chuckle over such felicitous *faux pas* as "rod iron" for wrought iron, and the red-nosed Rudolph's friend, "Olive, the other reindeer." And, almost invariably, we're warned somewhere in the piece to wipe those grins off our faces because, amusing as these malapropisms might be, they represent a treacherous trend, perhaps the ultimate triumph of television over literacy.

The latest of these ambivalent essays was by Graham Forst, an English teacher in North Vancouver. He gave us some truly knee-slapping examples of what I call fun-etic spelling–including the "rod-iron" rib-tickler–but sobered us up snappily with this admonition: "In sitting our children in front of the electronic baby sitter, we've created a generation of semi-literates, and their lack of respect for language can only reflect, or lead to, a lack of respect for tradition, or for thinking in general."

In fact the phenomenon is not restricted to children, and it's not new. It may be more rampant, but that's not because we're lazier and less literate. Far from being thoughtless, it represents an intricate intellectual process, and is an important and traditional element in the evolution of our language.

The metamorphosis of words through innocent mangling is known to philologists as "folk etymology." It's a natural and undeliberate inclination to cast obscure words or phrases into similar, but more logical and familiar, forms.

Take the "rod iron" example. As Mr. Forst points out, *wrought* is an all but obsolete past participle of *work,* and so is unfamiliar to the ear at first encounter. The natural phonetic rendering would be *rot,* but casual examination reveals the object to be made from rods. So *rod-iron* comes close in pronunciation, makes perfect logic, and may some day become the accepted dictionary word.

One of Mr. Forst's other examples–"cold slaw" for *cole slaw*–is already much more advanced along the folk etymology trail than might be realized. In fact, it may be that *cole slaw* is the variant form.

The American term comes from the Dutch *koolsla*, a truncated form of *kool salade*, or cabbage salad. *Kool* is the equivalent of our *kale* and the obsolete *cole*. Is it only coincidence that the Dutch word is so close to our *cool*, a sibling of *cold*, and that from the 13th to the 15th century, *cool* was often spelled *cole* in English?

The oldest citation for *cole slaw* in the *OED* is from a 1794 issue of the *Massachusetts Spy,* referring to "a piece of sliced cabbage, by Dutchmen ycleped [called] cold slaw." Of the four other citations, one refers to "coldslaugh" and the others to "cold slaw," including a recipe in Mrs. Rorer's 1886 *Philadelphia Cook Book.*

A favourite of folk etymologist buffs is the word *helpmate*. According to Genesis in some early Bibles, God figured the world might be a pretty lonely place for Adam, and said, "I will make an helpe meet for him," that is, a helper suitable to him. But the expression was widely misunderstood, and the imagined word *helpmeet* became a synonym for partner or spouse. Folk etymology ultimately changed *meet* to the more logical *mate*, and so we have the modern word *helpmate*.

Another of many examples is *shamefaced*, which was *shamefast* in Old and Middle English. Shame in those days was nothing to be ashamed of; it meant simply modesty or shyness. *Fast* in this sense meant fixed or lodged firmly, so the old word described a condition of demure reticence. By the 16th century *shame* had deteriorated in meaning, and was often accompanied by facial evidence of a stricken conscience. And now it's *shamefaced* that is lodged firmly in our vocabulary.

Not all the garblings fit the category. The "lost leaders" in a recent article about marketing, not Canadian politics, was just carelessness. So was the "for all intensive purposes" I saw in an office memo. Describing a moody young woman as a "pre-Madonna type" is probably something that will pass. But if you're confronted by an angry dog that's "a cross between a cocker spaniel and a datsun," it may be best just to grin and brazen it out. Certainly, you can't run away from it.

A lugubrious tome by Victoria Branden gives the impression that English has had it. The reader is the one who may have had it by the time he/she/him/her/they/them is/are through.

Unfairer than Fowler . . . and dead wrong

Unfurl the black crepe. Muffle the drums and beat them slowly. Rehearse the requisite requiem. We are about to have a funeral–for the English language.

Well, maybe it's not quite that imminent, but you certainly get the impression that the end is nigh if you read *In Defence of Plain English–The Decline and Fall of Literacy in Canada,* a new book by Victoria Branden, author, former English teacher, and highly wroth word-worrier.

The back-cover blurb on this lugubrious tome says: "This indispensable guide to the English language belongs beside the dictionary in every Canadian home." I can vouch for the second part. You'll need a dictionary to check some of the more idiosyncratic dicta.

And dicta there are. Ms. Branden's ruthless rulings on grammar, spelling, punctuation (" . . . 'like I said' won't do. You must say, *as* I said") make the prescriptive and pernickety H.W. Fowler sound linguistically *laissez-faire*. The subtitle might better be: Random Observations on Egregious Deviations from Victoria Branden's Rather Rigid, Often Quixotic, and Sometimes Exasperatingly Inconsistent Standards of English Usage.

A guide? One of the first things I looked for was

guidance on the issue of third-person, singular pronoun agreement–the he/she/him/her/they/them quandary that may be today's most pressing usage problem. In the absence of an index this wasn't easy, but I finally divined it in a chapter titled "Jargon, Gobbledegook and Bafflegab." Untypically equivocal, it says: "Must we interminably repeat he/she, or fall back on the ungrammatical 'their,' rather than use the convenient and conventional 'he' as an inclusive pronoun? I find it very distracting and annoying. And a nuisance."

So distracting, indeed, Ms. Branden uses virtually all the options at one place or another–" . . . a teacher who knows his/her stuff " (twice); "Everyone should read 'Here Lies Miss Groby' for themselves"; " . . . grammar taught by someone who isn't himself well-grounded in the subject"; and "no one dies because they are unfamiliar with participles."

The book does have some good bits. A chapter called "The Naughty Bits" is not one of them. To show how "gutter words now dominate our language and are in a fair way to extinguish all other vocabulary," Ms. Branden belabours the point by using variations on the four-letter word–in either her own prose or supporting citations–36 times.

She's at her peevish best when she rebukes the excesses of advertising, and the "Classyists" who use *utilize* for *use*, *simplistic* for *simple*, and "eck cetera." Her prime targets are the CBC, *The Toronto Star*, and *The Hamilton Spectator*, which are unlucky enough to be her main sources of daily intelligence. She says people who peddle words to the public have a special responsibility. I agree. She illustrates it with a perceived error in a book by Linda McQuaig. "Well, we all make mistakes," Ms. Branden says, "and Ms. McQuaig is a writer I admire just this side idolatry. But surely all those clever editors at Viking and Penguin should have caught it?" And surely the editors at Hounslow Press should have caught some of Ms. Branden's neck-snapping contradictions. At one point, for example, she scorns the use of *prior to* as "genteelspeak," and 20 pages later begins a sentence, "Prior to the language revolution . . ." And a simple dictionary check would have told the editors *critique* has served as a verb as well as a noun since the early 1700s, in spite of her stern diktat to the contrary.

She's at her eccentric worst with certain words. She urges us to look up *enthusiasm* in a good dictionary–"a most surprising word. I've hardly dared to use it since I looked it up." I looked it up in the *Oxford English Dictionary*, and found that it meant exactly what I thought it meant: A keen, animated, eager, maybe even passionate interest in something. An obsolete meaning is "possession by a god" or "supernatural inspiration," but Ms. Branden probably didn't mean that when she dared to use it in a chapter about school teachers. Just as, when she used *delicacy* in several places, she likely didn't intend the old meaning, "the quality of being addicted to pleasure or sensuous delights."

She proscribes the figurative use of *shambles* as a synonym for "mess" because shambles once meant "slaughter-house." If we wanted to get really fusty, we could point out that, before it meant "slaughter-house," it denoted merely a footstool, and then a table for displaying goods or counting money.

Ms. Branden is even deader wrong, or dead-wronger, when she states flatly that *odiferous* and *obstinance* are "unknown to dictionaries." They can be found, 36 pages apart, in Volume X of the *OED,* second edition. Also in the *Shorter OED*, and *Webster's Third New International* (1961).

These and several dozen other quibbles aside, the book really isn't as alarming as its title implies. Not everybody says "misanthorp" for *misanthrope*, or uses "smote" as the present tense of *smite.* And, notwithstanding Ms. Branden's rather haughty observation, some cab drivers are highly literate.

Here readers get to air some of their pet peeves, such as misusing the expression "to shoot oneself in the foot," and incorrect behaviour regarding aitches, aspirated or otherwise.

Bury my 'eart at wounded knee

At the risk of shooting myself in the foot–an hysterical rather than an heroic act–I'm going to let the readers take over, in terms of supplying the material.

John Holtby of Brockville gets his gaiters in a gnarl when people use the expression *shoot oneself in the foot* to mean doing something downright silly, usually resulting in some loss of face, rather than a toe.

As Mr. Holtby points out, the expression had a quite literal beginning. To avoid facing a fierce foe in battle, some soldiers shot themselves in the foot. This rendered them hors de combat and qualified them to use "handicapped parking" spaces upon their imminent return to Civvy Street.

But how did this activity metamorphose, metaphorically, from an act of poltroonery to one of buffoonery? Philip Howard in *Winged Words* speculates that cowboy movies had something to do with it. The paragon of horse opera oafishness was the hapless gunslinger who was too fast on the trigger and too slow on the draw, inflicting grievous harm to a pedal extremity and, for some reason, causing hilarity among audiences.

The changed meaning may also result from some

muddling with two other metaphors–to *put one's foot in one's mouth* and to *shoot off one's mouth*. Further confusing the issue is the common use of the phrase *foot and mouth disease*–a serious cattle disorder–to signify verbal blundering.

Ron Phillips of Winnipeg gets into an hypertensive snit when people use the two-letter indefinite article before words that begin with an aspirated aitch–as in *an hypertensive snit* or the two instances in the opening paragraph. Everybody knows the "rule": *a* before all consonants or vowels that have a consonant sound (universe, one, eunuch); *an* before all vowels or words that begin with a silent aitch (hour, honour, honest).

So why do so many people say "an unique experience" or "an historic event," even when it sometimes requires some diaphragmatic effort to do so? Who knows? It may be one of the hoariest holdovers in the language. Until some time in the early 12th century, when Old English was giving way to Middle English, there was no choice, and therefore no problem. *An* was the only indefinite article around. But *an television set* and *an cellular phone* didn't fall trippingly off the Middle-Aged tongue, so people began shortening *an* to *a* before sounded consonants. Not all people, however.

Speakers and writers who today use the longer article before a silent aitch are quite selective, whether they know it or not. Almost without exception, they do it when the first syllable of the main word is weak or unstressed. Thus, while almost everybody says *a history*, many say *an historian*. Same difference with *human* and *humane*. And those who say it usually write it, as in this passage from George Eliot's *Middlemarch* (1871): " . . . nothing was easier in those times than for an hereditary farmer of his grade to be ignorant." This is consistent, but absurd.

M. Barbara Byam of Toronto can't come to terms with the overused phrase *in terms of*. She sent along a raft (more like a garbage scow) of examples from federal government publications, CBC Radio, CJRT-FM university credit courses, and *Globe and Mail* clippings.

My guess is that an even more fulsome source would be the "debates" in any legislature in the country outside Québec. Verbal crutches of this sort are the stock in trade of politicians and other bombast-mongers in full rhetorical flight. They include *with respect to* and *in/with regard(s) to*, and the groan-inducing *let me share with the House*. But Ms. Byam says the habit is "making its insidious way out of academe and government and into the larger world." And she's right.

H.W. Fowler's (no longer) *Modern English Usage* says people probably use these oral aids as a substitute for punctuation. That may be true, but when it carries over into writing, mere idiomatic indolence becomes unpardonable sloth.

Anne Campbell of Regina noted that a recent contributor to the *Globe's* Cross Current column was identified as having "a degree in Chinese and German." She wonders where such a specialized language course is taught. May I suggest the University of Toronto, which also has a unit called "Special Services to Persons With a Disability." It doesn't say which one.

For centuries, we've been dropping letters from the ends of words. Which is why we now eat popcorn instead of popped corn, and say teen-age instead of teen-aged.

Teen-age and other mutant English terms

Somewhere there must be a kind of lexical limbo for lost letters and other mislaid bits and pieces of words. And many of its inhabitants are called *Ed*–or, more precisely and less formally–*ed*, and sometimes just *-d*.

English speakers for centuries have elided (from the Latin *elidere*, to crush out) or skipped over letters and word syllables, mainly because it makes certain combinations of vowels and consonants, or adjacent words, easier to pronounce. The practice often was reflected in writing, not just to mimic dialogue, but often to save handwriting time and effort ("y'rs truly"), and sometimes because pronunciation prevailed over grammar.

That last phenomenon has given us *ice cream* instead of *iced cream*, *popcorn* instead of *popped corn*, *teen-age* instead of *teen-aged* werewolves, and accounts for the surge in the population of *-ed*s and *-d*s in that verbal never-never land.

These severed syllables may be gone, but they're not forgotten. Although elision has gone on for centuries, it attracted attention lately in two noteworthy quarters: *Word Watching,* a newsletter published in Montreal; and *On Language,* a weekly words column by William

Safire in the Sunday *New York Times Magazine*.

Word Watching ran a letter from a reader complaining about a headline that contained the solecistic phrase, "it's suppose to be." The reader also noted elementary and high school students often speak of "old-fashion" clothing, and added that the practice makes him "wonder where our language is heading."

That reader is guilty of some old-fangle bias when he blames it all on teens and preteens (abbreviations that neatly avoid the *age/aged* problem). I doubt that young folk were the first to say *dome stadium*, or *ice tea*, or *middle age spread*, or *handicap parking*, or to place ads in the paper boasting of *knock-down prices.* I bought some "old-fashion summer sausage" recently in a supermarket, and "ice tea" is everywhere to be found on both lips and beverage menus.

So, young people aren't the problem. And the problem itself isn't young, if in fact it's even a problem. If our language is heading anywhere, it's the same direction it's been heading for a long time, with critics at every step of the way.

In a rather crotchety book called *Words and Their Uses–Past and Present*, written in 1890, American Richard Grant White dealt with the disgrace of *"ice-water* and *ice-cream."* "By mere carelessness in enunciation," he grumbled, "these compound words have come to be used for *iced-water* and *iced-cream*–most incorrectly and with a real confusion of language, if not of thought."

Confusion? Only in the unlikely event you were forced to make a choice between water dripping from a glacier, and water from another source, into which some glacier bits or other gelid lumps had been dropped. As for *ice cream,* what could it possibly be confused with, except maybe heavenly hash from a hypothermic Holstein?

Mr. Safire, considered by many (but not all) to be the final authority on English usage in this hemisphere, gives other examples of what he calls "stripped-down participles" acting as modifiers, including *corn beef*, *whip cream*, *toss salad*, *skim milk*, *barbecue chicken*, *candy apples,* and *stain glass*.

He quotes Professor John Algeo of the University of Georgia as saying that, "throughout the centuries, English has tended to reduce a group of consonants at the end of a word by losing the last one."

Still, Mr. Safire warns against letting careless pronunciation prevail. "Ears are sloppy and eyes are precise," he arbitrated, "accordingly, speech can be loose but writing should be tight. If it has taken a thousand years to lose the *b* in *lamb*, let it take a couple of generations at least to drop the *-ed* in the written *whipped cream*."

But he wants to have his bagel and eat it too, presumably with *ed*-less *cream cheese*, an elision that he feels has been sanctioned by time. He will not, however, countenance *process cheese*, or sleep in a *queen-size bed*. "You don't have to be a nut about retaining the *-ed* in print," he rules. "Let [language] change at its own good pace."

Which is precisely what it will do, is doing, and has always done, whether it's "suppose to" or not.

Some people have got it in for the verb "to get," even though it can have myriad meanings, including avoid, receive, possess, become, obtain, begin, and imply. Get the picture?

Getting in on the got/gotten debate

There's no getting around it. I've got to get around to the letter I got from Mrs. Toni Allen of Toronto, before it gets too late. It's already gotten yellow with age since it got to me in April. But I just haven't gotten the get-up-and-go to get down to brass tacks, get out from under the other stuff I've got to do, and get on with it, if you get what I'm getting at. But maybe I'm getting ahead of myself.

Mrs. Allen got to wondering about the verb *get* when she noticed *gotten* in two newspaper stories on the same day ("it's gotten worse" and "sweaters have gotten very expensive"). "It seems to be used instead of become," she observed, not altogether approvingly.

Wittingly or un-, Mrs. Allen has got/gotten herself embroiled in one of the longest logomachies in history. Disputations over the little word *get* and its past participle(s) make the Hundred Years' War look like a brief skirmish.

The Old English form *gietan* was only a word part, and the meaning was determined by the prefixes *a-*, *be-*, *for-*, *ofer-*, *on-*, or *under-*. Of these compounds, only *forget* and *beget* have survived, and the latter is getting a bit feeble. *Get* has not only become a word in itself, but has also acquired more meanings than all get-out.

There are at least a dozen senses in the first paragraph of this piece–including avoid, receive, possess, ought, must, become, arrive, obtain, develop, begin, understand, and imply.

Prepositions and adverbs have replaced the old prefixes as meaning-expanders (get at, get across, away, back, down, up, over, through, in, off, somewhere). Sometimes two are added, further proliferating the senses (get out of, get away with, get through to, down on, in on. I really get off on this.). Then there are compounds such as get-rich-quick, get-well cards, get-tough policies, get-ups, and getaway cars.

There are plenty more; the *OED* devotes 10 pages to *get* and its multiplicity of meanings and idioms. It became so versatile and ubiquitous by the turn of this century that many school teachers banned it, requiring their charges to choose more precise words such as *obtain* and *purchase*. Longman's *Guide to English Usage* (1988), still warns, somewhat irresolutely: "In really formal writing it is better not to use *get* very much."

Maybe the Longman people would have preferred it if Christ had said, "Move thyself behind me, Satan." And how would they recast Proverbs 4:7, which reads, "Wisdom is the principal thing; therefore get wisdom: and with all thy getting get understanding."

But what about the *got/gotten* dilemma? Well, theoretically it doesn't exist. Lindley Murray, the "father of English grammar," declared *gotten* obsolete in 1795. The *Oxford English Dictionary*, second edition, confirmed this in 1989 by saying it is "now rare except in *ill-gotten*" (although, oddly, it doesn't label *misbegotten* as obsolete or rare). *Webster* in 1864 opined that *gotten* was "obsolescent," and so have other American experts, one of them as recently as 1985. But *gotten* seems not to have heard, received, learnt, picked up on, or gotten the news. It's still very much alive in all English-speaking countries, though subjected to more tsk-tsking in Britain than elsewhere.

Certainly *gotten* has more seniority than *got.* Six centuries ago the present, past, and past participle forms were *get, gat,* and *goten. Gat* eventually became *got* by assimilation with *goten.* Then *goten* got both stretched to *gotten* and, by reverse assimilation, truncated to *got.* Get it?

Most dictionaries and usage books on this continent recognize both *got* and *gotten* as the participle. They usually mean the same thing, but there is a distinction in meaning between *she has gotten the job* (was the successful applicant) and *she has got the job* (is in that position). In other cases *gotten* might avoid confusion with odd-ioms such as *have got to* (must), and *have got* (possess).

The last word goes to Willard Espy, whose recent book *The Word's Gotten Out* has the funniest dedication I've seen. He says a friend argued for *Got* in the title, and another urged him to stick with *Gotten.* "After all," said the latter, "don't the Germans say Gotten Himmel?"

As the country rolled toward a referendum, the headlines became ever more bellicose. You could be forgiven for thinking we were heading for the trenches rather than the ballot box.

Constitutional reform? Fix bayonets!

"There has never been a war of Canadian origin, nor for a Canadian cause," wrote William Arthur Deacon, late, long-time literary critic for *The Globe and Mail* (and *Empire*) in 1933.

Well, there was one in the early days of the yes-or-no referendum–or so it strongly appeared, judging by the bellicose banner headlines brandished daily by our journals of record. Mind you, I didn't hear any rousing choruses of "Mademoiselle from Armentières." Nor did anyone, to my knowledge, come up with a really riveting rally-cry, like "Not necessarily conscription, but conscription if necessary."

But the familiar morning aroma of ink-and-newsprint was unmistakably mingled with the acrid odour of cordite, and the paragraphs were punctuated by whiffs of grape-shot, and often heavier ordnance.

We Canadians were verily at war, if the militant metaphoric maunderings of the headline writers and front-line correspondents were any indication. And, Mr. Deacon's kind and gentle characterization of us notwithstanding, it was a war of our own making, in a cause of our own creation: Constitutional Reform.

The battle was joined, of course, with the clarion call from the Charlottetown conference for a national referendum on the agreement reached by our leaders. Up to that point, according to the news coverage, the first ministers had been plying other figurative trades. One day they were busy little shoemakers, "cobbling together" the uppers and lowers of the agreement. The next they were brawny blacksmiths, "hammering out" one white-hot clause after another.

But those clausal ploughshares would soon be beaten into swords. The agreement was a spark to the latent, tinder-dry jingoism of our nation's newsmongers.

The Sudbury Star was one of the earliest enlistees. "The fight has begun in Quebec," an editorial advised, adding that "opponents of the accord will be rallying the troops to kill the package." Before long, the dispatches everywhere were bristling with the language of active hostility. "PQ targets unity deal," said *The Toronto Star*. "Battle lines drawn over the meaning of YES and NO," blared the Montreal *Gazette*. "The NO forces scored a direct hit on the YES forces today," intoned a Global TV Armageddon-caster.

Globe readers probably had some difficulty trying to figure out whether the war was ancient and religious ("Pro-Canada crusade begins"), colonial ("Battle of Quebec looms"), or of 20th century vintage ("Allies line up in Quebec"). Then again, maybe it was all a myth, as a story about Jean Piggot's retirement strongly hinted: "Just as Prime Minister Brian Mulroney was putting on his rhetorical armour . . . to confront the separatist dragons in the referendum campaign, one of the most savvy generals in the battle for national unity quietly retired from the field."

There were naval engagements too. Senator Patricia Carney vowed to "blow" B.C. Premier Mike Harcourt "out of the water" for his stand on female representation in the reformed Senate.

Mr. Mulroney got into the crossfire with his lamentable loose-lips remark about "enemies of Canada," after which the words "traitor" and "treason" seemed quite congruous. The *Globe* clarified matters by explaining that "the field of Mr. Mulroney's real enemies in this campaign has narrowed to two political parties–the Parti Québécois and the Bloc Québécois–and he is sharpening his rhetoric to do battle with both of them in the coming weeks."

The prime minister fired a dud, though, when he criticized Reform Party leader Preston Manning for relying on others to make up his mind for him. "I'll tell you," said the PM, "it's a good thing Winston Churchill didn't follow the Preston Manning school of leadership because the results of the Second World War might have been a little bit different." I had no idea Mr. Manning was that old.

Anyway, it all came down to this: On October 26, we besieged Canadians had to bite the ballot.

And that's not as opportunistic a play on words as it might appear. Our word *ballot* comes from the Italian *ballota*, defined by 16th century English lexicographer John Florio as "a rounde bullet." Before paper ballots or fancy voting machines, secret votes were cast by dropping either a white or black ball into an urn or box. Idle bullets were often put to this purpose. Somehow, it seems fitting, doesn't it?

For Reading, Reference, or Riffling

*

This is not a bibliography. To list all of the written works that may have served as references for this book, I would have to start somewhere just before *Dick and Jane.* A complete list would have to include restaurant menus, store signs, career ads, easy-assembly manuals, bumper stickers, T-shirts, health warnings, airplane streamers, vanity licence plates, and those posters that pop up at most major sporting events reading "John 3:16."

And, of course, whatever went into this book also represents a lifetime of being influenced, for better or worse, by the usual suspects–books, newspapers, and periodicals, not to mention all forms of the spoken, spouted, shouted, snarled, or whispered word.

If you've got this far–assuming you didn't skip everything to this point–I take it you're interested in some of the same things I am. What follows, then, is a highly selective list of books I enthusiastically recommend to your attention. I've left out some of the obvious ones, but I've included the *Oxford English Dictionary* and Fowler's *Modern English Usage.* I could have cited countless other dictionaries and many other usage books, but somehow I just couldn't see *not* mentioning these two. As for the rest, most are still in print, but some you will have to search hard for. They are all, in their own way, diverting and rewarding.

Baugh, Albert C.; Cable, Thomas. *A History of the English Language.* 3rd edition. Englewood Cliffs, N.J.: Prentice-Hall, 1978.

Berlitz, Charles. *Native Tongues.* New York: Grosset and Dunlap, 1982.

Bett, Henry. *Wanderings Among Words.* London: George Allen & Unwin Ltd., 1936.

Boren, James H. *When In Doubt, Mumble.* Toronto: Van Nostrand Reinhold Co., 1972.

Brewer, Rev. Cobham. *Dictionary of Phrase and Fable.* 8th edition. Cassell, London, 1963.

Burchfield, Robert. *Unlocking the English Language.* London, Boston: Faber and Faber, 1989.

Cobbett, William. *A Grammar of the English Language, Intended for the Use of Schools and of Young Persons in general; but more especially for the Use of Soldiers, Sailors, Apprentices, and Plough-Boys.* TO WHICH ARE ADDED, *Six Lessons, intended to prevent Statesmen from using false grammar, and from writing in an awkward manner.* Oxford: Oxford University Press, 1984. First published in 1823.

Copley, J. *Shift of Meaning.* Oxford: Oxford University Press, 1961.

Drabble, Margaret. *Oxford Companion to English Literature.* 5th edition. Oxford: Oxford University Press, 1985.

Enright, D.J. *Fair of Speech—The Uses of Euphemism.* Oxford: Oxford University Press, 1985.

Fowler, H.W. *A Dictionary of Modern English Usage.* Oxford: Oxford University Press, 1926.

Fowler, H.W.; Fowler, F.G. *The King's English.* 3rd edition. Oxford: Oxford University Press, 1931. First published in 1906.

Grose, Francis. *A Classical Dictionary of the Vulgar Tongue.* New York: Dorset Press, 1992. First published in 1796.

Hall, J.R. Clark. *A Concise Anglo-Saxon Dictionary.* 4th edition. Toronto: University of Toronto Press, 1991. First published in 1894.

Heller, Louis G.; Humez, Alexander; Dror, Malach. *The Private Lives of English Words.* New York: Wynwood Press, 1991.

McAdam, E.L., Jr.; Milne, George. *Johnson's Dictionary: A Modern Selection.* New York: Pantheon Books, 1963.

McArthur, Tom. *Oxford Companion to the English Language.* Oxford: Oxford University Press, 1992.

McDonald, James. *Wordly Wise.* London: Constable, 1984.

Mackay, Charles. *Lost Beauties of the English Language.* London: Bibliophile Books, 1987. First published in 1874.

Mencken, H.L. *The American Language.* 4th edition. New York: Alfred A. Knopf, 1937.

Murray, K.M. Elisabeth. *Caught In The Web of Words–James Murray and the Oxford English Dictionary.* Oxford: Oxford University Press, 1979.

Nurnberg, Maxwell. *I Always Look Up the Word "Egregious."* Englewood Cliffs, N.J.: Prentice-Hall, 1981.

Oxford English Dictionary. 2nd edition. Oxford: Oxford University Press, 1989.

Palmer, Rev. A. Smythe. *Folk-Etymology: A Dictionary of Verbal Corruptions of Words Perverted in Form or Meaning, By False Derivation or Mistaken Analogy.* Greenwood Press Publishers, 1969. First published in 1883.

Perrin, Noel. *Dr. Bowdler's Legacy: A History of Expurgated Books in England and America.* Boston: Nonpareil Books, 1992.

Ray, John. *A Collection of English Words Not Generally Used.* Aldershot, Hants., England: Scolar Press, 1969. First published in 1674.

Thomas, Lewis. *Et Cetera, Et Cetera–Notes of a Word-Watcher.* Toronto: Little Brown & Co., 1990.

Trench, Richard Chenevix. *A Select Glossary of English Words, Used Formerly in Senses Different from Their Present.* 2nd edition. London: John Parker, 1859.

——. *On the Study of Words: English Past and Present ["Supplée's Trench on Words"].* New York: A.C. Armstrong and Son, 1893.

Watkins, Calvert, ed. *The American Heritage Dictionary of Indo-European Roots.* Boston: Houghton Mifflin Co., 1985.

Webster's Dictionary of English Usage. Merriam Webster Inc., 1989.

Webster's Word Histories. Merriam Webster Inc., 1989.

Weekley, Ernest. *Adjectives And Other Words.* Freeport, N.Y.: Books for Libraries Press, reprint 1970. First published in 1930.

——. *An Etymological Dictionary of Modern English.* Toronto: General Publishing Co., Ltd., 1967 (2 volumes). First published in 1921.

——. *More Words Ancient and Modern.* Freeport, N.Y.: Books For Libraries Press, 1971. First published in 1927.

——. *Romance of Words.* 5th edition. London: John Murray, 1925.

——. *Something About Words.* London: John Murray, 1935.

——. *Words Ancient and Modern.* London: John Murray, 1926.

——. *Words and Names.* Freeport, N.Y.: Books for Libraries Press, 1971. First published in 1932.

Index of Words, Names, and Some Other Things

*